FISHING THE WILD WATERS

*An Angler's Search for Peace and
Adventure in the Wilderness*

CONOR SULLIVAN

PEGASUS BOOKS
NEW YORK LONDON

FISHING THE WILD WATERS

Pegasus Books, Ltd.
148 West 37th Street, 13th Floor
New York, NY 10018

First Pegasus Books cloth edition December 2021

Interior design by Maria Fernandez

The views expressed are those of the author and do not reflect the official policy or position of the U.S. Coast Guard or Department of Homeland Security.

ISBN: 978-1-64313-831-2

10 9 8 7 6 5 4 3 2 1

Printed in the United States of America
Distributed by Simon & Schuster
www.pegasusbooks.com

To Renee, you will forever be my ultimate catch.

Mom and Dad: The example you set was the most impactful influence on my life. Thanks for all those trips to the bait store.

CONTENTS

Foreword: How This All Began   vii

Chapter One: New England: Hallowed Waters   1

Chapter Two: Alaska: The Great Land and Even Better Fishing Spot   35

Chapter Three: Hawaii: The Proving Grounds   87

Chapter Four: Eating off the Grid without Going off the Deep End   133

HOW TO FISH LIKE A LOCAL

Appendix 1: Becoming a Fisherman   147

Appendix 2: Fly-Fishing   155

Appendix 3: New England   162

Appendix 4: Alaska   175

Appendix 5: Hawaii   202

Appendix 6: How to Care for Your Catch   218

Works Cited   225

How This All Began

My first memory is of fish. I was three years old and living in Charleston, South Carolina. My father and I were crabbing off a neighborhood dock and fishing for croakers. What I mostly remember was testing the claw strength of the blue crabs we caught, using every big stick I could find to poke into our bucket. I was fascinated by these crazy creatures we plucked from the sea. That was the moment a spark was lit and I became a lifelong fisherman. Almost every day since then I have either been fishing or figuring out how to get better at it. Fishing is at the root of nearly every important life decision I have made. I am fairly certain God put me on this Earth for two reasons: to fish and to teach others how to do the same.

There are a couple reasons for my obsession with fishing. The first is my dad. Tim Sullivan is a career Coast Guard officer who rose to the rank of a two-star admiral. If they handed out promotions for fish caught, he would likely be a cabinet member at the White House by now. He grew up in Wisconsin, fishing in local lakes and chasing down rabbits on foot for fun. His family and era looked to me like a scene from the movie *A Christmas Story*. He was an all-American boy and proof that anyone in this country can have a shot at greatness. He was and is still the best fisherman I have ever dropped a line with. He taught me and my two younger brothers, Rory and Patrick, how to fish as soon as we were able to hold a rod. These three individuals make up the inner circle of the best fishermen I know. You put the four of us on a boat, you will see a bunch of limits quickly filled. You will also likely hear grown men argue like children, complete with a few immature penis jokes, but I digress. My mom can discuss over tea the intricacies of setting a five-bait trolling spread for pelagics and has been known to tangle with a big halibut or two. Even my older sister, Maureen, who doesn't fish much anymore, can pick up a rod and work a stick bait for stripers without a break in the conversation. She has landed marlin and mahi-mahi off of Hawaii with me. She married a great guy named Hayden who also loves to hunt and fish. In short, we are a fishing family.

We are also a Coast Guard family. Growing up in a military lifestyle and eventually serving as a Coast Guard Officer myself has afforded me the opportunity to experience living in twelve different states, and I'm still counting. I consider it a rare gift to have lived in some of the best fishing locations in the country, and in the process, I have become a fishing pluralist of sorts. Living in so many states, each for about three years at a time, has allowed me to dial in at the local fisheries level in the oceans on both sides of the continent. By the time I was eight, I had already made weeklong trips into the Pacific, catching offshore species weighing way more than I did. By thirteen, I was working and fishing on local boats out of Niantic, Connecticut, selling stripers to adults who couldn't figure out how to catch any themselves, which in turn paid for my next trip out on the same head boat. When I wasn't doing that, I made trips as a sternman on a commercial lobster boat.

Now in my mid-thirties, I have served throughout this great country, holding unique jobs such as commanding a Fisheries Training Center in remote Kodiak, Alaska, and serving as the captain of a 110-foot Coast Guard cutter in the north Atlantic. The Coast Guard also sent me back to school, allowing me to earn a master's degree in marine affairs at the University of Rhode Island, all because my life still revolves around fish. I have a core group of close friends who share a similar view of the world, as well as my obsession: Josh Boyle, Brooks Horan, Dave Waldrip, Pat Murphy, and my best friend since childhood, Jon Dale, aka the fourth Sullivan brother. I clearly remember the day I met Jon. I was in seventh grade and fishing at the Pattagansett Lake boat ramp in East Lyme, Connecticut. I saw Jon walking toward the same dock I was on with his fishing rod in hand, and I thought to myself, "He is going to be my best friend." Since that moment, Jon and I have been as close as blood brothers. He joined the Coast Guard as well and we've had many great expeditions together as we've fished our way through life.

I have angled in most of the major fisheries in America and have an appreciation for all of them, but if I had to choose, it comes down to three "corners": Alaska, Hawaii, and New England.

I found Hawaii as a young boy, and New England in my early teenage years, but I had to wait until my nineteenth birthday to discover Alaska. New England is just a great salty place all on its own, where working waterfronts still exist among the creeping tide of gentrification. Hawaii and Alaska are the last two frontiers of fishing. They are full of danger, big fish, and extraordinary adventure. To fish these places is to reach back and stand alongside the first nation of fishermen—our ancestors—who plied the wild waters for thousands of years before us. With that in mind, fishing these waters can be a profound experience, demanding of our respect and reverence.

These three corners are both similar and different, and complement each other perfectly. Need a second opinion? In the case of Hawaii and Alaska, just ask the hundreds of humpback whales that swim the meridian lines between the two locales each year, reproducing in Hawaii and feeding on vast schools of fish in Alaska. The human residents of both places are equally as fond of the complementary aspects of the forty-ninth and fiftieth states, traveling between the two often and for similar reasons. New England, and by default our whole country, was founded and funded in no small part by fish, and in hallowed ports like Gloucester, New Bedford, and Point Judith, they still run on this natural resource.

So why do I fish? The fishing lifestyle is a lot of work for what could be picked up more easily at a high-end seafood shop. Realistically, there is no reason to chase down your own meal anymore. A mere dollar will buy all sorts of things at the closest fast-food restaurant. Frankly, most folks just do not understand why you would want to spend your time alone in the wilderness. With each passing year, our species's connection to our past's fishing roots grows weaker. Why do we need to get up at 3 A.M. anymore to catch the tide and get that limit of salmon?

Here is my take on why I pop out of bed when that Saturday alarm breaks the silence long before sunrise breaks the horizon: I believe that quietly in each of our souls, beyond the sarcasm, past the consumerism and daily grind, lies dormant a different side of us, the real side of us. For me, it's the realization that I feel more alone in a congested city than twenty miles offshore. I feel an intrinsic connection to the world beyond the one that humans created, and I want to maintain that. Both for my inner self and for preserving these open waters for my children and beyond. On the practical side, filling a freezer with salmon and halibut, which provides my growing family with the world's healthiest protein—truly wild caught—just feels right. Of all the waters that I have fished, Hawaii, Alaska, and New England are those special places on Earth where I can pull back the curtain, connect to the sea, and gaze into my own soul—the soul of a fisherman.

Although there are plenty of "how-tos" in this book, I am not writing it as a basic primer on the sport and craft. I am not writing it as someone who has fishing all mapped out in these great expanses of water. I am not the professor instructing his charges on where to drop a line. I am writing this book for the fisherman, the man or woman who scrutinizes the often-limited fishing section of any bookstore, hoping to find more, and for the folks who will walk up to strangers fishing off a pier while on a vacation to peek in their bucket and start a conversation. This book is for the men and women who read how-to guides on hook types and Palomar knots with passion and are ready for something that teaches the technical and then maybe transcends it. It's for those anglers, my kindred spirits, who use fishing as a vehicle to escape from their daily grind and find themselves with a beaming smile as they walk down the path toward their favorite fishing spot early in the morning.

My desire to transfer my fishing stories to paper is due in large part to being the son of a professional writer. My mom, Teresa, was born in Scotland. Her family followed the American dream, arriving in New York Harbor on the ocean liner the *Queen Mary*, and she is my inspiration for putting down my fishing rod once in a while and picking up a pen. She raised four kids, often on her own when my dad was at sea, but kept writing. With a deployed husband, she had a major article published in *Time* magazine. In her late fifties, she applied and was accepted into UCLA's graduate School of Theater, Film, and Television, and spends nearly every day writing screenplays. That takes drive. Mom, I am fully certain I will never be able to write like you, but I know I feel the passion that you feel.

One final note: being able to go out and explore the far reaches of the sea comes at a price—an opportunity cost, if you will. I count my lucky stars that I married a woman who not only tolerates my passion but encourages it. Renee, this book is one big thank you. As Eddie Vedder put it, "If ever there was someone to keep me at home, it would be you." Thank you for allowing me to chase dreams of fish, but you are by far my best catch. Anabelle, Brayden, and Will, you have re-taught me the simplest joys of living. I couldn't imagine my life without all of you in it. We have so many adventures ahead of us.

To the rest of you, let's get to it.

Chapter One

New England: Hallowed Waters

All I felt was a slight pinch as the tuna kicked up its tail and sent the serrated knife through my left hand, slicing it open, beginning at the webbing between my thumb and pointer finger and ripping it right down to about the middle of my palm. I looked down in a moment of detached awareness and observed that the inside of my hand was hollow between the palm in the front and bone on the back. That void quickly filled with blood, which was flowing down my arm and onto the deck. I was alone, fifteen miles offshore, and in trouble. Checkmate.

The phrase "big game hunting" invokes an image of a hunter battling for life or death with a large and often dangerous animal. For better or worse, the image of big game fishing seems to always invoke the angler subduing a spirited, yet physically harmless fish. Make no mistake, when you hook a marlin, halibut, or tuna, it is usually a fight to the death for one of the two parties involved. For those of us who pursue these fish off smaller boats, the risk that you could actually get hurt in the process goes up remarkably. I learned this truth the hard way, fishing in the giant tuna capital of the United States: Gloucester, Massachusetts.

My first encounter with bluefin was fishing with Dave Waldrip on the famed southwest corner of Stellwagen Bank. Dave, a retired Coast Guard officer, had invited me, my dad, and my brother Patrick out on his thirty-one-foot Eastern boat named the *Relentless*. I had recently moved to Gloucester and had one goal in mind: to become a bluefin tuna fisherman. Dave had commercially fished for tuna in his earlier days and was now running a very successful charter business, but he wanted to take a fun trip out that day to introduce us to the fishery. We had launched out of Green Harbor, Massachusetts, in search of the tuna. Perched high above the water on the flying bridge of the boat, we trolled the waters while scanning the horizon for breaking fish or bird activity. As we pushed farther out, we saw exactly what we were looking for: tuna on the surface. Dave maneuvered the boat to have it pass ahead of the fish while our lures ran right over them. I expected the fish to turn and attack the rubber squids on the spreader bars with reckless abandon, but instead they didn't seem to pay much attention to them at all. I was dumbfounded. As the day went on, we encountered similar situations—hundreds of tuna surrounding the boat, but none willing to feed. It was both impressive and maddening at the same time. No matter what lure or technique we tried, the results were the same. These fish were not like other species. They were smart and extremely finicky, and I was hooked.

First things first: If I was to live and fish out of Gloucester, I needed to get onto a boat. Although we almost always owned a boat growing up, and my professional career revolved around being on them, ironically, buying my own was a big step. After a few months of searching, I settled on an older, but reliable 1988 Invader: center console, single engine, single battery, with just a few soft spots in the fiberglass deck. Although it lacked curb appeal, it was a heavy, over-built hull and the price was right. This was my ticket to getting offshore to the tuna grounds.

I spent the next season cutting my teeth on bluefin fishing, chalking up some near misses and lost fish, but I felt confident that I was going to have some success in the fall. My dad and I hooked one a few weeks earlier, fishing in some snotty weather while trolling on Stellwagen. It was a wild and sketchy ride just getting out to the bank due to the seas that day. We took a few good waves over the bow, but slowly picked our way through them out to the area. Unfortunately, that fish came off during the fight, but we were getting it all dialed in.

Every summer, bluefin migrate from the Mediterranean Sea and the Gulf of Mexico to the cold waters of New England. Like whales on their annual migration to Alaska, the mission is simple for tuna: pack on as many pounds from the rich bait-fish stocks. From June until November, bluefin are everywhere and nowhere. A clandestine fish that doesn't stop swimming, they will never be exactly where you think they are. At times, giant bluefin will be calmly swimming below the surface, showing no interest in feeding, just sightseeing. Other times, they will explode out of the sea, chasing bait and striking any lure presented to them. It can be a maddening fish to pursue, and I have spent many trips working waters that seemed to teem with everything but tuna. My focus was on learning to predict their movements and intercept them. Like anything else, the more you are out there, the more you begin to feel the pulse of the ocean. Summer had passed. With the cooler winds beginning to blow and the days getting shorter, it was evident that the crescendo of the fall was about to occur, and I positioned myself right in the middle of it.

Although living in the acclaimed fishing location of Gloucester, I actually didn't have a lot of friends who enjoyed running offshore in a small boat to burn gas trolling tuna all day, so I ended up fishing alone more often than not. I was comfortable with it—maybe too comfortable—and enjoyed the challenge and solitude.

I pushed off on another solo run early one Sunday morning in October. On the last several trips I hadn't seen fish around but I knew it was just a matter of time until they came back over the bank again. Success equated to putting in the time out there. That morning I motored out of the harbor well before dawn and was making turns toward Stellwagen as the first sign of the sun began to appear. The fishery had become very popular—and this was before there were TV shows about it. I wanted to get out to the grounds before the weekend warriors made the bank a parking lot. The weather was calm and the sky overcast, and I had a good feeling that today was the day. As it turned out, it was the day, but not the one I had envisioned. My gear was simple, with the primary tuna feed being sand eels. I decided to forgo trolling the iconic spreader bar with bulb squid, and instead trolled a single nine-inch sluggo. Yes, those freshwater bass baits, when rigged with a sturdy hook and 150-pound fluorocarbon, looked deadly in the water.

I started at the northwest corner of the bank, where the bottom contour came up to ninety feet, and followed the birds and depth contours from there. Working to the southeast, I finally saw what I was looking for—crashing tuna. The white water stood out against the gray water and gray sky. These fish have a tendency to fleetingly surface and then disappear, so I quickly made my way over to the action, then slowed to four knots to set my trap, trolling my bait through the area where I had just seen them. Right on cue, I heard the wonderful ratchet sound of the reel dumping line. I calmly slowed the boat, made my way to the rod, and began the battle. Initially, I let the fish run, while I figured out how to battle it. I first tried fighting it from a dead stop for about an hour. On a small, pitching boat by myself, I didn't like "stand-up" fighting the fish. Realizing that this technique was not yielding progress, I stationed myself amidships on the starboard side and slowly followed the fish, alternating between reeling and driving while sitting down. This was easier on my legs and back, and it felt like I was making a little progress. I managed to bring it up to the surface at about forty yards, and was able to get a good look at it. It was a good-sized fish, but it quickly sounded before I could get it any closer to the boat. It held its ground at ninety feet below. I followed the fish around the boat as it circled, but I couldn't lift it. It soon became apparent that this fish wasn't moving, and the only one tiring was me. I stopped the boat and drifted with the fish. Hours began to pass and nothing changed. I was becoming frustrated and even more tired as I leaned back against the rod expecting it to start moving toward the surface; but it didn't. At six-four and weighing in at a solid two hundred and twenty pounds, I should have been able to put the screws to this fish with this short stand-up rod, built for applying maximum torque, but it wasn't working. I just couldn't gain an inch on this fish.

In evolutionary terms, a bluefin tuna is the most advanced fish species out there. Everything about them is designed for speed and efficiency. The sickle-shaped tail is made for pure power, the small finlets located between the tail and the dorsal/anal fins are there to help maneuver the fish without using the tail, which would sacrifice energy. Their oversize eyes are completely flush with their head, which is hard as cement. The circulatory system of the bluefin employs a counter-current exchange that allows the heat generated by the muscles to warm its blood, enabling it to efficiently operate in cold waters that other tuna cannot. And they get big—real big. While the rod and reel record is just over 1,400 pounds, bigger ones are out there. To hook one is to hook into a freight train.

And that's exactly what it felt like. At hour four, with all my drinking water gone, I was feeling the effects of exhaustion and likely the early signs of dehydration. I was reacting slower and had pure task focus with no awareness of what else was going on. I even questioned if I was still hooked to a fish or if I was just snagged on the bottom at this point. I needed a new plan.

I stopped the engine, trimmed it up, and put the rod in one of my stainless steel, angled rod holders, making it nearly horizontal to the water. With a slight breeze I was able to keep the fish upwind of the boat and drift with it. From this position, I locked the drag down on my Penn 6/0 Senator reel, put a glove on my right hand, dropped to my knees, and began to fight the fish like I was giant tuna fishing. The rod was fully bent to the waterline, a perfect parabolic arch, and the eighty-pound line had to be at its breaking strength. At this point, I would have been secretly relieved if the line snapped. This amount of constant pressure was enough to move the fish, and it began the iconic slow circles up toward the surface that tuna are known for. After another hour, I finally had "deep color"—seeing the fish below—and with a few more circles managed to get it boat-side. I had not been hallucinating: it was a tuna, and a good one at that. Leadering with my right hand, I gaffed the fish cleanly in the shoulder with the other. It was a relief. The fish did not fight anymore; it seemed to be as tired as I was.

By this point, I was definitely dehydrated and spent. It took everything I had to lift the fish up and pull it backward over the gunwale. I stood still for a moment, staring at it. The iridescent blues and silvers along its back were beautiful. I couldn't believe I had finally caught one. After this herculean fight, I wanted to shift focus to taking care of the fish. The blood of a fish, especially an athletic fish like a tuna, is filled with stress hormones, heat, and, if not removed, bacteria. To properly bleed a fish, you have to do it while the heart is still beating. What I regretfully did not do was stun the fish first. With a razor-sharp serrated knife in my now weak left hand, I cut the fish at its gills and then did something I hadn't done before or since: I made a cut at the caudal peduncle (base of the tail) to sever another blood vessel. Due to my position, I held the knife blade-side up as I leaned across the fish's back to make the final cut.

And that was when the tuna kicked up its tail and sent the serrated knife through my left hand. The slice went from the beginning of the webbing between my thumb and pointer finger and went down to the middle of my palm. My hand was almost ripped in half, and in that moment, I could now see the bone in the back. Blood was flowing into the hole, and I was alone, fifteen miles offshore.

The first words out of my mouth were, "I didn't just do this!" But, yes, I pushed myself so hard and so far with my tunnel vision of landing that fish that I didn't even realize it until the ocean said, "Checkmate." I was in trouble, and my next snap decisions would prove critical. I grabbed the first thing I saw to stop the bleeding, which unfortunately was a dirty glove soaked with sweat and fish slime. Part of my palm was now on the back of my hand. I avoided looking at it. I tried to catch my breath and take inventory of my situation: I had cut my hand in half. I didn't know if I had cut any major blood vessels. I didn't feel light-headed yet. I also didn't see any other boats. Man, I wished that parking lot of weekend warrior boats was still around now. Knowing what a loss of consciousness would mean, I swallowed my pride, calmly picked up the radio, tuned into channel 16, and put out a request for assistance.

A sailboat heard my radio transmission and diverted toward me. As luck would have it, there was a nurse on the boat. As we closed on each other's position, they put over their dinghy and the nurse came onboard. She calmly removed the glove covering my hand and gasped. Her initial reaction was, "You might need a helicopter." "Absolutely not!" was my response. I couldn't bear the thought of having to be hoisted by a Coast Guard helicopter. She confirmed that I was in rough shape but, once again, luck threw me a lifeline in the form of a Massachusetts Environmental Police boat, who had also diverted to my position. They offered to drive me back to a waiting ambulance while the second officer followed behind in my boat. This was not how I expected this day to go.

I called my then-girlfriend, Renee, from the back of the ambulance, asking her to give my family a heads up that I was ok. I had to be taken to a hospital with a specialty hand surgeon. My mom later told me that when she saw Renee's number pop up on a Sunday afternoon, she knew something was wrong.

I imagine it was quite a sight for the medical staff to see when I was wheeled into the emergency room wearing orange Grundens, covered in sweat and blood, and probably not being the most cooperative of patients. I was wearing my favorite hooded sweatshirt and was sad to see the nurses cut it off of me. I can remember Renee walking into the room to let me know she was there. She then looked at my hand. The nurses told me they found her in the bathroom, trying not to pass out from the sight. With the serrated knife cut going through the web of my hand and down toward the base of my palm, there was a decent pile of leftovers in what I recall was a hospital's version of an ashtray, which was not a pleasant sight to see.

With a hand full of stitches, the surgeon discharged me that evening, and I made my way over to my boat to tow it home and recover the fish. As I walked over in the dark, I saw this large tail jutting out of a fifty-gallon barrel. Some good Samaritans had thankfully iced the fish down for me. It was too big for the barrel though, and the tail portion extended into the air like a cactus. With my nondominant hand (I'm left-handed), I began the process of filleting the fish and icing the loins of meat in my cooler. When it was complete, with some help, we threw the carcass into the water. I just stood there, staring at this magnificent frame of an animal who only hours before had wrecked me. It was not a feeling of accomplishment or pride, just of respect and a touch of sadness. I was the victor but not by much.

At the end of the day, I was very lucky. Only by the grace of God did I escape permanent damage or worse. A few milli-meters more and I would have severed key nerves to my thumb. Despite sawing through my hand, by a miracle, my tendons were intact, and although I had a literal handful of stitches, I went on to make a full recovery within a few weeks.

By the time my hand was healed, I only had time for one more trip on the boat that season. I wanted to end that year on my own terms before winter and went out to catch a few cod. The knife accident changed the way I fished, though: It made me much more serious about my trade. Bad things happened to others, but not me—until that experience. It was easy to point the finger at fishing alone as the culprit. While having a partner would have eased the battle, the very same thing may have occurred. I had to plan out future battles more closely. Rather than gaffing a large fish, I built a harpoon to safely stick the fish before it came in the boat. I bit the financial bullet and invested in higher quality rods and reels, with two-speed retrieves that could lift a fish from the depths. I also purchased a first aide kit. Offshore fishing wasn't a game, there were real consequences to face, and I was damned if I was going to ever let that happen again.

Gloucester was a good fit for me. An hour drive north of Boston and at the tip of Cape Ann, it is technically an island, both in geographic and metaphoric terms. It is a town that has sidestepped the gentrification that, from a fisherman's standpoint, plagues much of New England. This town has produced generations of fishermen that have worked along the same waterfront, braving the worst of the north Atlantic to make a living doing something that is in their blood. It remains a working town with grit and soul where nearly everyone has a connection to the sea or those who work it. Its waterfront is not littered with chain boutiques, but rather marine supply stores, ice houses, and fish processors. It has a certain energy to it, knowing that just beyond the Dog Bar Breakwater, a wild and exciting world full of fish and adventure awaits. Looking back, it reminded me of Kodiak, Alaska—another reason why it felt like home. Gloucester holds the title of America's oldest seaport, and the harbor is busy with boats gearing up for their next trip, or offloading from their last, as it has been for hundreds of years. Sitting at the doorstep of an incredibly rich ecosystem, the relatively shallow water of the continental shelf extending off-shore from Gloucester is among the richest in the world. While its commercial fleet harvests a multitude of species, there is one fish that will always be at the top: the Atlantic cod.

Associated with fish and chips, fish sticks, and any recipe where white, flaky fish is desired, cod is America's choice in fish. Like chicken, it has a mild flavor and takes on the taste of what you put on it. The country, and the world, has grown a taste for it. The oil from its liver—cod liver oil—has been taken as a dietary supplement for generations, and my mother recalls being forced to swallow a spoonful a day as a kid. This fish is in the family Gadidae, along with its less famous cousins haddock and Atlantic pollock, and all three are often referred to as groundfish, due to their constant proximity to the sea-floor. They are a cold-water fish that is mostly located in New England waters throughout the year. Cod played a major role in the early economy of the United States and continue to feed it today. If you have eaten cod, chances are good you have had cod from Gloucester.

I started fishing for cod as a thirteen-year-old in south-east Connecticut, which in modern times is considered the southern part of the species' range. Even back in the early 1990s, cod stock was in a tailspin, a victim of overfishing. It was apparent that I was fishing for scraps after decades of huge catches and was a hundred years too late to the party. Back then I would jump on a local eighty-five-foot head boat called the *MI-JOY* out of Niantic, Connecticut, where I often filled in as a quasi-spare deckhand. At thirteen, I cleaned the boat, gaffed fish, sold refreshments to customers, and untangled lines, all in exchange for the ten-dollar fishing trip. Additionally, running a little side gig, I could usually sell a portion of my catch to anglers who didn't do as well to pay for the next two or three trips. We used to call these anglers "Hartfordians," in reference to the landlocked city of Hartford whose anglers would come down to the ocean to fish, but did not always know what they were doing. It was a slick little deal I had going and it kept me on the water. In the winter and spring, well before the stripers and bluefish arrived, which was the bread-and-butter fishery, the boat would fish for cod south of Block Island or Montauk. This all-day trip was a big adventure in big water for a young angler. In hindsight, in those pre–cell phone days, I can't believe my parents trusted me enough to be dropped off at 4 A.M. on a Saturday to go fishing all day, often by myself, in winter. But that same freedom allowed me to grow into my own. As a teenager, I wasn't getting in trouble hanging out with the wrong crowd because I was too busy hanging around with gruff old guys with weathered faces who would pass down stories of cod fishing, all while chain-smoking cigarettes. To this day, the smell of tobacco on a cold day smells to me like cod fishing.

Those winter and spring days at sea were brutal on a young kid, and I got sick a lot. The fishing was not great either. Over three seasons I probably caught only a handful of keepers, but I was undeterred. In fact, the first cod fishing trip I ever made one January with my dad and Jon Dale was a rude awakening to the harsh life of a fisherman on the north Atlantic.

I distinctly remember listening to the marine forecast the day before and bravely, if not ignorantly, responding, "Eight-foot waves aren't that big." Sure enough, we were in for some winter weather. The three-hour ride out to the grounds took my morale from sky high to the deck plates. Even my dad, who at the time was the commanding officer of a two-hundred-and-twenty-five-foot ship, was not loving the ride. I was throwing my guts up, and by the time we stopped to anchor, I could barely make my way to the cold rail to drop down my double clam rig. Most of the day consisted of me languishing inside and occasionally stepping out to try to fish for a bit. Jon, on the other hand, was having a great time. He seemed to have his sea legs about him and ended up pulling up the pool-winning cod (largest fish on the boat), a nice fourteen-pound fish. All I had was a dogfish and someone else's small cod to show for the effort. I am pretty sure that lifting someone else's fish also cursed me for years to come.

Any sane kid would have walked away from this once and for all, but there was something about this brown fish with white spots that kept bringing me back. Even as a kid, I recognized the historical significance of cod and used to love perusing any historical literature I could find about them. Cape Cod was named after the species and the Isle of Shoals off of New Hampshire was named after the shoals of cod that were once plentiful around them. Records of individual cod well surpassing one hundred pounds were documented. This fish was the backbone of the colonial economy and fed the world. I used to love reading old stories by Tim Coleman, a renowned New England fisherman, as he pursued the species in the colder months of the year. He plied the same waters south of Block Island as I fished, and filled the boat with massive fifty-pound fish that seemed to attack his jigs with reckless abandon. Based on how the current fishing was, Coleman's accounts were like reading a fictional story set in actual places.

In southern New England, the cod were essentially gone and didn't seem to be coming back, victims of overfishing and particularly bottom trawling. A typical day of fishing yielded perhaps fifteen keeper cod for twice as many anglers, none of which often reached double-digit sizes. The stock was simply exhausted, and we were just picking away at the leftovers. The old-timers would tell tales of the fishing up north, on places like Georges Bank, Tillies Bank, and Stellwagen Bank, and filling the boat with whale cod (a term to describe the biggest of cod). I would lay on the bench trying to sleep as we steamed three hours out to the fishing grounds, thinking about what it would have been like to have seen fish like they described, and how I wished I had been around years ago to experience it all. The day's trip would likely consist of fishing all day to have, if I was lucky, one bite from a cod, which would usually be too small to keep. But over a decade later, now having found my way to Gloucester as a grown man, I had finally reached these hallowed waters that those old-timers had told me about, and I wanted to see if they still held fish. This was my chance to find the cod.

Stellwagen Bank, in addition to being a bluefin tuna magnet, was the premier springtime cod spot off Gloucester.

The crescent-shaped bank, located due south from Gloucester, rose up like a mountain to within ninety feet of the surface. The cold, nutrient-rich water is forced up the water column, colliding with the sides of the bank, where it mixes with the sunlight-soaked surface water to encourage rich plankton growth. This creates an incredibly prolific base of the food chain that all other ocean species benefit from. The area teems with sea life of all sizes. I had times on Stellwagen when whales would unexpectedly surface next to me, so close I could smell their fishy exhales, on the hunt for their own meal. I worried they would capsize me and not even know it. Seabirds would fill the sky like smoke as they chased baitfish on the surface, while the whales, tuna, and cod attacked from below. Stellwagen was no secret, though; every angler from Gloucester to Cape Cod who had a seaworthy boat would fish it or had fished it for the last four hundred years. The pilgrims had likely sailed over it on their way to Plymouth. Stellwagen was a fine cod-fishing spot for me. I would drift along the slopes of the banks, work a jig, and feel the sheer joy that is a cod attacking it. It was refreshing to land these market-size cod with regularity. They did exist and were still in catchable numbers. But following a tip from a local friend led me to quite possibly the best cod fishing I would ever know.

Rather than running the fifteen miles south to Stellwagen, I found a piece of bottom that was comparatively inshore. The fishing was only good during the first hour or two of the day, when the cod and haddock seemed to be aggressive on this small hump on the seafloor. By the time the sun came up, the bite slowed down, so I would strive to be on the water by 4 A.M. and anchored up with lines in the water by the time the first streaks of sunrise broke. This usually meant the alarm clock would go off at 2 A.M. As the sun began to break, I had my own little piece of the good old days, feeling as if I was in the old-timers' stories as I pulled cod over the rail. For a few months each year, nearly each fish that came up was a wall hanger by today's standards and would have been considered a monster during my youth. While all of my cod in southern New England were well under ten pounds, this spot would provide numerous twenty-to-twenty-five-pound fish. It was incredible. I kept the place a secret and only took my brothers and dad on these excursions. Stories or photos were not shared outside the circle of trust; some spots are just too important to talk about.

Compared to fishing for other species, catching cod was simple. You either used bait, usually clams, or diamond jigs. A diamond jig is an elongated metal lure that flutters like a dragonfly when jigged. Growing up, getting a fish to hit a jig was the ultimate challenge. This was because it was what the guys in Tim Coleman's stories used, as they employed the "iron clam" as they sometimes called it, to boat cod hand over fist. I would study the black and white photos of his whale cod, with a sixteen-ounce jig hanging out of the fish's mouth, as I read his stories over and over. I knew the big fish wanted the iron clam, but the fish in southern New England didn't seem too interested in it. However, it was a different story up north. Working an old school Norwegian-style jig or something a little flashier like a butterfly jig was the right answer on many days and felt more rewarding than fooling one on a clump of clam.

Spring began, and my spot was producing fish. I would slip out a few times a week to jig the area and routinely picked up nice cod. Fishing gets better in Gloucester in early summer, which coincided with my younger brother Patrick coming into town while he was home from college in Santa Barbara. It was time for a trip together to see if we could make a little magic happen.

He slept on the couch at my place. There was not much sleeping involved as we were up around 2:30 A.M. and, with the boat already hooked up to my truck, we exchanged minimal words as we climbed in and trailered it down the ramp and motored out in the darkness, well before dawn. We had to take it slow in the dark, using a spotlight to make sure we didn't run over any lobster pots as we pushed out of the harbor and toward the grounds. Watching the depth finder, I saw what I was looking for, the small rise in the bottom contour that held schools of cod. I swung the boat back up current as we quietly lowered the anchor and settled in. I put a little chum in the water to attract any cod in the area to our location as we rigged up our rods. By this point, the first signs of sunrise began to show in the east. The chum was working—a school of mackerel took up residence underneath us. It actually took some work to get our large cod jig through the school and down to the bottom, as the mackerel would attack the jigs with abandon as they dropped. As we started jigging close to sunrise, my lure got nailed by something big. It was one of those fish that made you shift the rod from under your arm to the top of your thigh to keep up with it. I lifted it off the bottom and started gaining line. It still felt big. I kept calm and did all I could to be perfect in this fight. Cod will often get foul-hooked when jigging, so you never know how good of a hook set you have. I just kept constant tension and was gaining line methodically. We watched it circle up from the depths, and as it came to the surface, I saw the biggest cod my eyes had seen in the flesh, a solid forty-pound fish that fought as valiantly as any cod could. After all those years of reading about fish this big, I finally got one. Pat gaffed it neatly in the shoulder and hoisted it aboard. It was a fish that I didn't know still existed.

Pat cut a mackerel that we caught earlier in half and gently lowered it down to the bottom. The sun was up now, and the bite felt like it was slowing down, but I was hoping there was one more whale cod down there for Pat. I never told him, but I said a quiet prayer for Pat to hook up. Maybe Saint Peter was listening because Pat took a big hit. He too seemed surprised by the power of the fish. He kept the line tight and the pressure constant. This was a monster. His rod was bent over and he was in for a battle. Looking down, I could see the white of its belly in the depths of the water as it circled up the last twenty-five feet. As Pat later told me, he knew it was a monster because I got very quiet as I waited for it to come in from visual to gaffing range. With a quick pull, the biggest cod I had ever seen was hauled onboard.

We called it fifty pounds, but it might have been bigger; I wish we had weighed it. Neither of our fish were even close to fitting into the cooler. It was more than enough fish, so after boating Pat's monster, we called the trip. Weighing anchor, we returned back to the boat launch by 8 A.M., and it felt like we were riding a golden chariot into Rome. The boat ramp was busy as most fishermen were still in the process of getting their boats off the trailer and readied for points well offshore. We asked a fellow fisherman to take a picture of us once we recovered the boat. The look on his face said it all. That morning, we launched at 4 A.M. and took a ride back to the early 1900s for a few hours. After a lifetime of searching, in one glorious predawn moment, I had found the cod.

As I write this book, the recreational retention of any cod is now severely limited north of Cape Cod. The species was collectively fished so hard that even taking more than one right now is too much for the species to bear.

A must-read book for cod fishermen is aptly titled *Cod*, written by Mark Kurlansky. In it, the author describes with impressive detail how this one fish played a pivotal role in both the discovery of America and in starting the economic engine of our country. But when he described modern cod fisherman as being "at the wrong end of a 1,000 year fishing spree," I knew, unfortunately, it was true. Unfortunately, it is true. Just over one hundred years after fishery managers declared that the ocean could not be fished out, we proved them wrong. While I got a taste of the good ol' days, I will never know what it was like to fish for cod and have them so abundant that an angler could fill their boat to the gunwale with them. The phrase "shifting baselines" is the scientific term to describe the reset that each generation has on the relative abundance of a species. As the oral history of those cod from Tim Coleman's days begin to fade away, so does the understanding of what was once there. I may soon be the old-timer talking about the last of the whale cod to a young angler.

Fisheries management in New England is not an easy subject to discuss. The regulations have gotten tighter each year, but the groundfish stocks have not rebounded as hoped. The limiting of quotas, permits, and days at sea produces divisiveness, winners, losers, and heartache. Unlike forestry or other terrestrial management of resources, the management of fish involves never actually seeing what you are managing. Additionally, managing fish really means managing fishermen. A reduction in the quota is a reduction in livelihood. Everything from a car payment to preschool tuition is paid for by fish, and I empathize with men and women who work the sea for a living. It is a dangerous and daunting way of putting food on the table, and I am always impressed by their courage and work ethic.

Seafood is realistically the last commercially available wild protein. The sale of wild, terrestrial meat has been banned for one hundred years and those wishing to eat wild must generally go out and capture it themselves. However, seafood is different. Even at fast-food restaurants, a fish sandwich is often from wild-caught fish, typically Alaskan pollock. This is actually a rather amazing feat. Humans have not yet been able to make an artificial ecosystem that is as productive as the seas, and this form of wild food is still readily available to the masses. Through practices such as organic farming and grass-fed or grass-finished beef, top dollar is paid to have domesticated food mimic its wild food counterpart. However, the ultimate free-range choice is an animal that is allowed to eat what it chooses and travel potentially thousands of miles without ever passing through a human hand until its capture. Commercial fishermen are the last of the hunters, and Gloucester is the epicenter of the last of the New England game.

Every time I trailered my boat to the public boat ramp, I passed the Man at the Wheel monument, the iconic statue of a fisherman leaning on a ship's wheel located along Gloucester's waterfront. Beneath the man is a plaque that lists the names of every lost Gloucester fisherman dating back hundreds of years. Driving past it, I realized that every single one of those men intended to come home from their trip.

The north Atlantic is unforgiving. Whether you catch fish or not, whether you return home or not is an unknown and often mysterious ratio of luck and skill. It took cutting my hand nearly in half for me to fully learn this lesson. I understood that the sea is not a playground. At best, it is indifferent to you. But the allure of it is too much to turn away from, and for thousands of years, fishermen have tempted fate by plying its waters in search of big fish. Running a boat, often by myself, was rewarding but also, at times, a grind. When the fishing was good, I would get home in the afternoon, prep the boat again, make a few sandwiches, and get to bed, ready to do it all over a few hours later. When I needed a break, I hung up my boat keys and got out my surf caster.

Running a boat involves a day of preparation beforehand. Ice needs to be loaded, oil levels checked, and something is always broken. Whether or not you were successful, the workload was about the same and at times it seemed like the boat owned me. But the opposite of this is surf casting, the pursuit of fish from the shore along the New England coast. Through the generations, specific rods and reels have been created for this technique. Long rods, sometimes over twelve feet in length, paired with large spinning reels allow anglers to launch lures far out into deep water. With just a few items needed, all of which can fit into your pockets, it is weightless compared to the burden of a boat. There are no checklists or ignition sequences. Rather than being hundreds of feet above your query, it is up close and intimate. More akin to bow hunting, it is elegant hand-to-hand combat that levels the playing field and makes it a fair fight. You have to enter into the fish's turf without getting swept off a rock, and battle a fish which knows every snag and ledge in the neighborhood.

By the time early fall would roll around in New England, I always kept my surf casting gear in my 4Runner—just a rod and a few select lures—so that at a moment's notice, I could be down along the coast, moving fast and light along the rocks, sling shoting iconic lures into the frothing white water of Cape Ann. I was in pursuit of one fish: the striped bass, arguably the premier inshore fish on the East Coast, although nobody calls them that. In the Chesapeake Bay they are called rock-fish, farther north they are stripers, the old salts call them line sliders, and for those who earn a living catching them, they are simply bass.

The species is a modern-day success story of fisheries management and proof that we can both ruin a species and practice redemption by restoring them. The once-healthy stock, which spawns primarily in the Chesapeake Bay and Hudson River, was decimated in the 1960s and 1970s, due to habitat destruction and overfishing. By the 1980s, the stock was in peril. But something remarkable happened. Through the implementation of strict catch limits, and reduction of pollution and habitat destruction, the fish came back. Catch and release fishing, something that was a foreign concept in the past, also took hold.

This was a species that I grew up fishing for up and down the East Coast. My first striper was likely caught bouncing bucktails off the Chesapeake Bay Bridge pilings as my dad and I took turns casting off of our family boat. Later on, we would drift in swirling tide rips at the mouth of Long Island Sound, known as "The Race," using eels at night, or pursuing them at the top of their range in Gloucester and New Hampshire on hand-carved plugs. Stripers are perhaps the most accessible saltwater gamefish to much of coastal America, keeping in mind there are even stripers on the Pacific coast and in inland lakes. On the East Coast, from the bottom of their range in North Carolina, up to the Canadian border, esoteric, regional techniques have been developed to chase them. In New England, however, the traditional, most addicting, and often hardest way to catch stripers is surf casting.

The concept of surf casting is as old as fishing itself; working lures carved of wood, or now plastic, along turbulent shores by heaving them into the wind and surf from long, strong rods that can reach beyond the breakers. Casting live eels or fishing cut bait on the bottom is generally the most successful technique for shore fishing and is a feat to be proud of. I really enjoy these techniques and will never be too proud to fish cut bait on the bottom. To capture a large striper on a lure is something else though. It takes skill and dedication, and it is a fish well-earned, something to be proud of. But to land a large striper surf casting with a homemade lure was a great achievement for me growing up, and still is, attesting to sufficient mastery in several categories. I am dedicated to the pursuit.

I started making my own lures at a young age. I distinctly remember my dad coming home with a fly-tying kit when I was about seven and both of us taking a turn on creating one that evening. His, as I recall, looked perfect, while mine was an accurate replica of a small dust bunny. I received a six-weight fly rod for a Christmas present at age nine and taught myself how to cast, and even got pretty good at roll casts. Gathering feathers and fur from all sorts of sources, including our pet dog, I taught myself how to tie elk hair caddis flies, mickey finns, and woolly buggers. It was self-sufficiency for a kid who couldn't buy his way to success, and the immersive experience made actually catching fish with my own ties just a little more special.

In high school, life and the Coast Guard took the family to Cleveland, Ohio, for a few years. Initially disappointed to be separated from the ocean, I soon discovered the impressive steelhead fishery that existed in the waters of Lake Erie. This fishery became a proving ground for my ability to tie salmon and steelhead flies and it wasn't long until my dad, brothers, and I were only using my own flies to catch double-digit weight fish. This fishery also prepared me for fishing in Alaska, where many of the same patterns for Steelhead were equally effective on Pacific salmon. Most of my later salmon were caught on patterns created in that same fly vise.

In those early years I would take branches from a tree in my yard and shape them with my pocketknife. Using any paint I could find in the garage and using eye screws to hold the hooks, I began surf casting these wooden surface poppers. I can remember hooking a large bluefish off the beach in Nantucket as a young teenager on that tree limb lure and feeling this intense sense of pride as a result of it. Carving wooden lures, whether they be archaic tree limb poppers or tantalizing swimming plugs decades later, became a passion. With a block of wood and hand tools, drilling, grinding, and shaping lures that exactly met the specifications I needed was the complete opposite of anything available commercially. I would spend two weeks at times fashioning, from my own hands, amid the flying sawdust particles, the single, unique lure to match the one I had already designed in my head.

For the biggest stripers, serious surf casting is reserved for nighttime and a few hours on either side of the sun, and the best time of the year is in the early summer and then again in the fall. The bottom line is this: to get a striper of consequence from the shore on a lure, you will have to earn it, and you will probably get cold, wet, and tired doing it. But it is fun!

After running hard for several weeks on my boat, I decided I needed a change in pace. It was time to see if I could connect with some stripers along the coast. I am a firm believer that there is a direct correlation between the amount of self-inflicted misery you put yourself through and the number of fish you catch. Rather than just get up early, I was up well before dawn, climbing along the rocks and listening for the next set of waves to come in as I made my way to a few choice spots. Armed with a headlamp and ice cleats (to hold me to the rocks), I eased out onto a desolate point and launched out a homemade white and yellow pencil popper. I had turned this lure in my workshop a few months earlier. Through the process of shaping it, I was also adding life to it and could tell it was a winner. I had never casted this lure before, so on that dark morning, I was unsure if it was alluring to fish, or just me. To work any lure in the dark is to really interpret what you feel through the rod and "see" it in your head. Each pop of the rod would make the lure's front half slap the surface and skate either right or left momentarily. The rhythm of this retrieve is what I was seeing through the rod tip's vibrations.

The first brush strokes of orange on the horizon perfectly backlit my plug as it skated across the surface. I was taking in the beauty of it all when the ocean exploded around it, leaving a giant white hole where once there was a lure, as if it had hit a mine. I was on! The striper took a good run, but my twelve-foot, old-school Penn–surf caster rod was doing its job. Hooking any big striper off the rocks makes your brain simultaneously contemplate fighting the fish and figuring out the riddle of where and how to land it. I was perched relativity high on a rock so the angle of my line kept it above most bottom snags. After a long run, which seemed to never end, I was able to use the crashing breakers to guide the fish into a suitable landing spot between two big boulders. The key to not losing the fish at this crucial moment is to keep tension on the line. Easing down to the water's edge between waves with my rod outstretched behind me, I grabbed the fish by its gill plate and quickly retreated to higher ground. At forty inches, it was the biggest striper I had ever caught surf casting. It was a proud walk back to my car. The sun just broke the horizon as my trip was coming to an end. To get the fish on a homemade plug made it even more special. I ended up harvesting this fish and enjoying it for many meals.

With these fish, or at least the big ones, being mostly nocturnal, I went home and took a nap, but wanted to try it again that evening. Same spot, same lure. I casted for well over an hour without a sniff. Right at sunset, something amazing occurred. I sent out the plug for another retrieve, a school of baitfish called bunker (large menhaden) appeared out of seemingly thin air around my plug. The lure popped once more and momentarily snagged one of these two-pound baits for a split second. As I processed what had just occurred, the bunker and the pencil popper disappeared. I was tight again with a monster striper. It was another colossal battle, but the fish stayed perpendicular to my spot on the rock, making it an epic but enjoyable fight. I finally eased this beauty to the shoreline, admired it for a moment, and let it go. It was one of those magical moments that happen when you spend enough time doing what you love.

A decade later I found myself back in New England for several years, living in Portsmouth, New Hampshire. Stationed on another Coast Guard cutter, I would use the sea as both a workplace and place of rest. An hour up the coast from Gloucester, I was now in the heart of northern New England, an area of iconic scenery and seemingly limitless habitat for striped bass. The seacoast of New Hampshire is relatively unknown to fishermen outside of the local area. While Cape Cod is known for its summer homes and summer traffic, and

Maine is likewise a popular vacation area for much of the Northeast, coastal New Hampshire, probably a product of being so small, is left alone. If you drive fast, you might miss the couple exits that will take you to a beautiful coastline where stacked lobster traps are a common sight in yards, and everyone seems to have a connection to the sea. For a surf caster up for a challenge, this was the place to be.

The seacoast of New Hampshire is well above the center mass for stripers. The migration from their natal waters of the Chesapeake, and to a lesser extent, the Hudson River, is a long swim from New Hampshire. The cold waters of the Gulf of Maine are slow to warm and therefore are last to receive migrating stripers and first to lose them. While the abundant amount of bait will entice stripers, the cold water will eventually signal to them that it is time to head toward warmer waters. Farther south, much ado is made of the "fall run," in which huge schools of stripers and bluefish congregate and blitz the likewise huge schools of bait. However, northern New England does not often get this level of mayhem.

The fish of northern New England are what build up the mass of the fall run farther south. It seems like the fish are there one day and gone the next. The fall blitz lasted only one day this particular year, and just my luck, that was the day I took off from fishing to sight in my rifle ahead of deer season! And while plenty of big fish are caught up north, personally speaking, there seemed to be a much larger amount of smaller schoolies present, and relatively few "cow" stripers that are caught farther south. So much of the New Hampshire coast also appeared to be premier striper habitat since nearly all of it is comprised of large boulders and relatively deep water. There was no crowding of anglers for the few coveted spots. If I saw someone in an area I wanted to fish, there was always a new spot to try.

The goal for me that season was again to land a keeper striper on a homemade lure. A New England winter is the perfect time to shape lures in the basement. With three young children, and Renee catching up on her favorite show after the kids were put to bed, a few hours each evening was the perfect amount of time to use a knife, chisel, and sandpaper to reduce an ordinary wooden dowel into a piece of functional art. That winter I set out to make two lures, which I would mostly rely on for the upcoming season of fishing: a pencil popper and a Danny swimmer. Both are top water lures. Pencil poppers, long and narrow, slap the water with their face as they dance across the surface. They are the perfect lure to prospect an area quickly while also raising any fish that may be around. They are my lure of choice; just enough action to stand out, but not enough to overdo it, like dancing at a wedding. Danny swimmers, named after the legendary lure maker Danny Pichney, are a much slower lure. With a metal lip, they slowly waggle across the surface and appear to be an easy meal for a passing fish. I added small pieces of weight to perfectly ballast and orientate the lures, and they were ready for color. Yellow and white are tough colors to beat for stripers and both lures were given the same iconic paint job. Even without casting them, I knew these lures would produce.

By June, the schoolie stripers began to flood into the area. I started to prospect new spots along the coast and Piscataqua

River, which separates New Hampshire from Maine. My scouting led me to a rocky point that jutted out nearly fifty feet at low tide and was completely submerged during high tide. Creating a tide rip when covered, this area allowed stripers to ambush bait flowing over the rocks without expending much energy. It was a fishy spot and I spent the morning there. With no action on the pencil popper, I switched to the Danny swimmer. The lazy motion of the lure was too much to resist and soon a striper came crashing into it. It was a typical schoolie, about twenty-four inches or so, but the first of the year and also proof that the lure was a winner.

As the season progressed, both lures continued to produce, with fish crashing them with wild abandon. One strike looked more like a shark attack, with the striper coming directly from beneath and doing a backflip after the strike. But larger fish were more elusive. This seemed to be the trend that season: a lot of smaller fish, but keepers were just not showing up.

Following an extended Coast Guard deployment that took me up to Greenland and into the Arctic Circle, I returned home to catch the last of that year's striper season. Coincidentally, Patrick, my youngest brother and now an Air Force officer, returned home from his Middle East deployment on the same day as I returned from the Arctic. He came up to visit for a week and we set out to do some surf casting. While out in search of a suitable surf break, he found a rocky point with a good break that changed from a rock to a pebble beach. Being a fisherman himself, he knew this spot would hold fish. A quick midday trip here confirmed our suspicions. We connected with a few small schoolies. If small fish hung around here during the day, big ones would surely make their presence known after hours. After Pat left for his next duty station, I kept fishing this spot.

The season was beginning to wind down; fall can be a quick season in northern New England. I began fishing after dark and again at sunrise as much as I could. Unlike in my younger years, I did not have an abundant amount of time to throw at the challenge. Fishing with three kids is a zero-sum game, however, lucky for me, stripers prefer the night shift. So, with the kids in the upstairs windows waving, I would often venture back out after bedtime to chase my quest.

It wasn't on fire but at least every other trip resulted in either a strike or an undersized fish. I thought I had the fish I was looking for one night, working a swimming plug in from a cast. I took a big strike close to the beach. By the power of the run, it was obvious this was a far bigger fish. The surf was up that night and even with my headlamp on, I couldn't gauge where the waves were at with anything but my ears. My timing must have been off because as I eased the fish through the breakers, the lure came flying back at me.

I was spending nearly every other day working the coastline during those remaining weeks. The winding down of the season puts a level of anxiety on fishermen, the days left to fish slip quickly away, like sand in an hourglass. I really wanted to connect with just one striper of consequence before they were gone. With the help of an ever-patient wife, I once again began my weekend at 5 A.M., tiptoeing out the door to cast the now-weathered plug back off my rocky point. That morning I stopped off at a new spot for sunrise, but the gamble didn't pay off. It was evident that the seasons were shifting as the cold northerly winds made me pull up my hood and blow into my hands to warm them a little more.

Back into the car and down to Pat's spot. With the protection of the rocky point, the waters inside the cove were calmer. With fresh line but tired lures, I launched out the same pencil popper once again to have it dance in the waters of New Hampshire. Halfway back on the retrieve, a fish struck the lure. It was one of those strikes that was meant to consume and not to sample. It was immediately obvious this was a bigger fish compared to the numerous schoolies I'd caught earlier in the season. I did everything I could to be perfect, the rod was at the correct angle, I didn't horse the fish nor did I give it too much slack. Time slowed and I just wanted to land it. Timing it with the smaller waves, I surfed it out of the water and onto the rocky beach, then quickly scampered down and secured my catch. I had done it. It was a perfect slot limit fish, between twenty-eight and thirty-five inches, as per the regulations, with my battered pencil popper hanging from the corner of its mouth. I knew it was my last one of the season. I would take a few more trips, but deep down, I could tell it was the buzzer beater.

Standing on that rocky beach in the darkness of late October, launching wooden plugs far out into the darkness as I searched these waters for a bite, my mind wandered back in time. With Portsmouth being founded in 1623, there had been four hundred years of surf casters, maybe more, working this same spot, and many more for hundreds or thousands of years before them. The tackle had changed but the pursuit was the same. We tend to view history as frozen in time, battles fought long ago or people who just exist in textbooks. But on that night, history felt closer. I could picture early American settlers casting from this same rocky point with tarred cotton cord and hooks made one at a time by a blacksmith.

While I fished to feed my soul, that angler was likely fishing to feed his or her body. We were pursuing the same fish and probably carved wooden lures with the same anticipation of a large striper crashing through the breakers to inhale it. The lineage of it all brought it home for me. I was on the leading edge of generations of surf casters for but a moment in time. The striper I caught that night provided several wonderful meals for my family. That fish fed our bodies and was the perfect way to start a dinnertime fish story for the next generation of my young anglers.

New England will forever hold a special place with me. The history of the land, the still relative abundance of the fish, and the cold gray water are quintessential to the modern angler. With proper conservation, there will be a future fisherman plying the same waters, wondering what it was like to fish here "back in the day." To fish New England is to connect with our past and gain perspective on things. Although the land has been settled since the 1600s by European settlers, the sea has never been tamed. Just beyond the old stone walls and small towns lies a frontier that relatively few come to meet. The cold and often stormy sea holds within it untold stories of nightmares and dreams come true of fishermen who took a risk to seek their fish. The aura of early American excitement and opportunity still lingers. The fishing locations are historic, the fish are big, and the sea will forever be unforgiving.

Chapter Two

Alaska:
The Great Land and
Even Better Fishing Spot

F ew have been able to adequately capture the grandeur of Alaska in words. To see limitless ranges and miles of coastline completely void of human traces is rare nearly everywhere else in the United States. I am confident that most fish I caught in Alaska had never seen a hook until they came across mine. Experiencing Alaska put into perspective all the other aspects of my life; its sheer enormity seems to minimize small, personal problems. It also holds a mirror, illuminating the many self-imposed restrictions we put upon ourselves. As one old coastguardsman put it, "It's a land so beautiful, it hurts your heart."

To live in Alaska is to rebel against the modernity of the rest of society. It represents a willing transfer of material convenience for personal freedom. Jack London could not have set *The Call of the Wild* in any other location but Alaska, because here, the wild isn't a tidy plot of land set aside for recreation. Here it is practically a whole state, the forty-ninth. And more than a geographic area, the "wild" of Alaska is just as much a state of mind. This area of vast, untamed wilderness boasts more coastline than any other state in the country, and has the lowest population density in the country. It is both the most western and most eastern state, earning the latter by crossing the international dateline via the Aleutian Islands. The population center is Anchorage. Beyond that, the towns begin to quickly look more like outposts, with many accessible only by sea or air. Even the capital, Juneau, has a road system that just . . . ends. Alaskans are an incredibly self-reliant people. There is a limited safety net from both a social and a life-or-death perspective, and to thrive you have to have the life skills and the courage to find a way to overcome problems on your own.

Alaska is a very welcoming, friendly place where you can do nearly anything, except snag a salmon in a river. The reason being that much of Alaska's value is derived from its wildlife. In terms of money, fishing is one of the highest grossing industries in the state, with thousands of fishermen and hunters traveling thousands of miles to fish its wild and majestic waters. The tightness of the game laws reflects the intrinsic value that Alaskans place on their wildlife. In hunting, there is a concept called "fair chase." It is an exceptional idea that advocates giving the animal a level playing field as well as carrying yourself in a manner that is respectful to the animal and your fellow hunters. Some examples of fair chase include not taking a risky shot, avoiding the killing of an animal when it is vulnerable or disadvantaged (like ducks sitting on the water), and utilizing the entire animal once taken. It is a code of conduct that true hunters abide by.

Alaska weaves ethics and fair chase into their fishing regulations. Here are a few examples:

- Only one rod per person and not more than two hooks on that line.
- No snagging of salmon in fresh water.
- Only certain species of fish may be used as bait.
- No high grading (throwing small fish back to swap out for a bigger fish).
- No fishing upstream on certain rivers in the summer in order to allow salmon to spawn.

With the American frontier closing sixty-nine years before Alaska became a state, it was the last place teeming with wild game and fish. Having witnessed the demise of the Atlantic salmon and Atlantic halibut, it seemed that the Alaskan territory was the last chance for fishermen and fishery managers to get it right.

The mistakes of the past amplified the importance of preserving Alaska. Being confronted with extraordinary biomass of fish during a short season, fishermen feel the mutually exclusive motivations of wanting to catch every fish they can, while also knowing this level of abundance only exists here. If the salmon disappear from Alaska, they are doomed everywhere else.

It is just in this last generation or two that this great land came into the trust of the United States government, and it is fascinating to be so close to history and meet old-timers who remember it as a territory. Generally speaking, there are six major areas in Alaska: Southeast, Southcentral, Southwestern (Aleutians), Western, Interior, and the Arctic. While I have been fortunate to travel the state from the Arctic Circle out to the Aleutian chain, my heart belongs to Kodiak Island in Southcentral Alaska. Located two hundred and fifty air miles south of Anchorage and about the size of Connecticut and is home to approximately 3,500 Kodiak brown bears and twice that number of humans, it is a huge island archipelago with a small human population. To put it into perspective, if Kodiak was your hand, the road system and town would fit in your thumb nail.

I first visited Alaska just before my eighteenth birthday. I was due to report to the Coast Guard Academy in July, and my dad took my brothers and I for a trip to the northland before my report day. It was an eye-opening experience. We drove throughout the Kenai Peninsula pursuing salmon and halibut during the time of year when the sun never sets. Blowing out rental-car tires, fishing for halibut in big seas, and drinking from a glacier exposed me to a land that I didn't previously know existed. The freedom we all felt would soon be a juxtaposition to the regimented lifestyle I was about to enter.

I came back to Alaska nine years later to visit my close friend Josh Boyle on Kodiak Island. Josh is perhaps the best backcountry hunter and woodsman I will ever meet and is one of those rare men who was born two hundred years too late. Bad luck for the Lewis and Clark expedition, but I am really glad I got to call him a roommate, friend, coworker, and groomsman. After we graduated together from the Coast Guard Academy, he went to Kodiak and was not looking back. On his second assignment to Kodiak he invited me up to experience it. Josh lived in a small cabin near the banks of the Russian River. I could walk down the hill to the river and catch pink salmon until my arm fell off. I slept on his couch with an elk hide as a blanket, wanting to get up as soon as I could to get back outside. That trip to Kodiak ignited a fire in me that was inextinguishable, and I was determined to find a path back.

Fate has a funny way of sorting things out. Less than a year later, while vacationing with my parents and then-fiancée, Renee, in Florida, my cell phone rang. It was a 703 area code so I knew it was the call from the personnel "detailer" in Washington, DC—the individual who issues out orders and assignments for officers. I discreetly excused myself from the mini-golf game we were in the middle of. The conversation went like this: "Hello, Lieutenant, this is Lieutenant Commander Whoever. I would like to offer you command of the North Pacific Regional Fisheries Training Center, in Kodiak." Me: "OK, sounds good. Just curious, do I have any other options?" "Nope." And that was it. Returning to the mini-golf game quietly, my dad sniffed me out somehow using his admiral-sense and asked, "So what did the detailer say?"

Renee and I got married that summer and we were in Kodiak a week later; in her case it was a literal leap of faith. Our wedding song, "Come Away with Me," was not just a metaphor. We were Kodiak or bust.

There was no better place to be newlyweds. We were thousands of miles from family and had to look inward for strength and support; our love and trust grew deep roots as a result. Sundays didn't involve trips to a shopping center or wine tasting, but rather roll casts and mountain hikes. We learned to avoid bears and park into the wind so car doors wouldn't be bent backward in the winter hurricanes. Life was simple and patterned by the seasons and weather. I was mesmerized by rivers literally chock-full of salmon, with their backs out of the water, all fighting to move upstream and away from the bears. These were pinks and chum salmon. For those who are less familiar with the five species of Pacific salmon, not all are created equal.

You will notice that every salmon species has an official name and at least one common name depending on your geographic location. They are kings in Alaska, chinooks in Canada and the Great Lakes, and blackmouths in the Pacific Northwest. Generally, a region will only call them one name. You could call a king a chinook in Alaska and everyone would know exactly what you meant. They would also assume you are either a Canadian salmon fisherman or a Hartfordian.

Here is the list of salmon, with their Alaskan name first:

1. king (chinook)
2. silver (coho)
3. red (sockeye)
4. dog (chum)
5. humpy (pink)

I must point out, however, that these titles are by no means a cut-and-dried or settled list. In fact, the mere action of me trying to assign one name for each salmon type sent my buddy Brooks and me into a heated debate, with Brooks even coming up with references.

It is completely feasible that all five species can spawn in the same river. Biology has assigned each species an arrival time so that there is not excessive competition for the runway. The kings are the first to arrive, often beginning in May and pushing in until July. Immediately behind them are the reds. Although in the river at the same time, the reds are focused on reaching a lake, and generally hug the shoreline, as compared to the kings who like to stay in the deep.

Once those two runs dry up in July, the pinks show up along with the dogs. It's not hard to determine if the pinks are in. Their numbers are staggering and will fill a river to the point that there is not enough room for them all. The dogs are big, but less common. It is easy to pick them out among the hordes of pinks as they look like brown submarines with beautiful purple bands along their flanks. Finally, in mid-August, the silvers arrive. These fourth-quarter silver bullets come in just as the days begin to get shorter and the mornings colder. I have caught them dime bright into October, and even caught spawned out ones around New Year's! There are only a few months in the year in which salmon are not available in the rivers of Alaska.

Kings are the king, plain and simple. These powerhouses have brought me to my knees in praise and sorrow. They are by far the largest of the entire Pacific salmon genus. The largest sport-caught specimen came out of the Kenai River, topping out at just under one hundred pounds. They have been caught commercially over the magical hundred-pound mark but not on rod and reel—yet. They require larger, deeper rivers for spawning: the Kenai, Yukon, and Stikine produce these fish. On Kodiak, only two rivers produce natural kings: the Ayakulik (eye-ya-cool-lick) and Karluk (car-luck). Additionally, successful stocking programs, using fish from the Karluk system, have stocked multiple Kodiak road system rivers.

In the most simplistic terms, the two methods to target kings are from a boat or in the rivers once they begin to run. Kodiak, by virtue of its location in the Gulf of Alaska, supports what is referred to as a feeder king population, meaning that fish of various year classes, from all west coast rivers, feed and grow in this area. An angler could catch kings every month of the year, which is a completely achievable undertaking if you are brave enough. Spring and early summer are when you would expect your largest fish to appear in the area, as these bruisers travel past Kodiak from the Bering Sea, Aleutian Islands, and Alaskan Peninsula, all bound for their spawning rivers.

My close friend Brooks Horan (already mentioned for the great salmon-naming debate) taught me to become a better salmon troller. He is a Coast Guard Captain and endodontist for the service by trade. He was a fisheries biology major as an undergrad, but he came to realize that he could do far more fishing as a dental specialist than as a fishery scientist and decided to go to medical school. A great outdoorsman and an even better friend, he is the perfect example of the modern hunter and fisherman.

Brooks's play for king trolling is similar to that of tuna trolling. Start where you found fish last and look for bait, birds, and whales. Whereas silver salmon often ride higher in the water column, kings generally hang closer to the bottom. There are no absolutes, but my best days of trolling were when we constantly jockeyed the downrigger to keep the presentation fifteen feet off the bottom. Downriggers: that's right, salmon trolling is downrigger trolling. Our usual depth of water was between 70 and 160 feet, and there is just no productive way other than downriggers to keep your bait down that deep while trolling. If you have the money, get electric downriggers, but more important than anything else is to ensure you have enough wire or braid on your downrigger reel; Brooks and I used cheap rentals one day and were, shall we say, sadly (*%#!@*!) dismayed when the spool stopped at forty-five feet!

If you have never been obsessed with lure colors, you haven't trolled for kings. I never really bought into owning six different shades of green for a hootchie—salmon fishermen's term for rubber squid skirt—but all it takes is one day where UV green gets hit way more than double-glow green, and all of a sudden you are dropping sixty bucks at the store, buying everything made by Silver Horde, one of the primary salmon lure manufacturers. There is a group for people like that, they are called King Fishermen and we meet at the Kodiak Brewery every Friday night.

The White King

Fishing Log: 13 September

One 35 lb. king, one silver. Buoy 4. Small, purple Ace Hi. Awesome! Post-work troll. 75 feet down in 90 feet.

"Fish, fish, fish, starboard rod!" I glanced back to see one of our rods pop tall off the downrigger release and then slam back down under the strain of a big fish. I ran back to the rod and, without taking it out of the holder, reeled hard for a few cranks until line started peeling off the reel. My friend Bill Burwell and I had gone out for a quick post-work troll off Kodiak one September day, and things were looking good. It was a bluebird day; the sun was out and the seas were calm. It was the last of the summer weather and I wanted to use every opportunity left to land another king. This species had gotten deep into my being. I couldn't stop thinking about my next opportunity to tangle with another one. Today was that day, and we were tight to a good one. We had one small silver in the cooler, but this second hit was something entirely different.

Bill cleared the other rod while I held on tight. With a big fish like this, all you could do on the first run was to hold on and hope that the hook and leader held. Once the cockpit was cleared and the fish settled in, I handed the rod off and took over the helm as Bill went to work on this big king. It tried all the knee-shaking tricks indicative of a big fish: running at the boat, rolling over the leader, and diving toward the props, plus a few monster runs for good measure. Knowing this was the fish of the season for me, I laid out a net, gaff, and harpoon. Keeping slight starboard rudder on, I saw the dim glow down deep slowly working up toward us. I went with the net as I ran back and forth from the helm to the starboard corner.

The moment between seeing a fish of this size and having it within the range of the net lasts about nine hours. Every head shake, every tail stroke seemed like it was in slow motion and created a deeper sense of anxiety, since the longer this scene lasts, the higher the odds that the fish wins. The euphoria of sliding the fish into the net undid all those fears. Seeing that fish laying on the deck—for a moment, all I could do was stare. It was the biggest king I had ever seen.

This fish was a white king. Due to a genetic anomaly, about five percent of king salmon have white flesh. According to the Alaska Department of Fish and Game, white kings cannot process carotenoids, which are found in crustaceans like shrimp, that make the flesh of other salmon various shades of red. There are variations on white kings, which range from a red/white swirl known as "marbled" to a more ivory white color. They also taste great. King salmon are delicious; white kings are mind-blowingly amazing. Its rich, buttery texture is something that cannot be forgotten. I can remember the first time I had Renee try some. She took a bite, smiled, and told me to only catch these from now on. We both laughed because of the statistical challenge/nightmare that would present. I did well that summer, though, almost like a dream come true, a whopping eighty percent of my Kings were white! If Alaska had a lottery, I would have bought a ticket. I was on fire. When not trolling the coastal waters in pursuit of white kings, I was in the rivers calmly searching for the reds.

If I took a moment to think about what one place in the world would be considered my "happy place," that place where I close my eyes and find comfort in, it would be pursuing reds in a quiet river, armed with just my fly rod, waders, and a pair of polarized glasses. I have battled reds in numerous watersheds, but my favorites are the ones in which I get to sight fish. The fish don't stop long to rest in most rivers, so to be consistently successful depends on your ability to predict their movements based on river conditions, then you locate them and present your fly. Their slate gray and blue camouflage is impressive; against the similar-hued river rocks they practically disappear. Staring at millions of cubic feet of water coursing by, I realized over the years that my eyes tended to notice either the faint blue of the fish's tail or simply the absence of seeing the river rocks. Only then would I be able to see the rest of the fish.

With just the sound of the river rushing by and an occasional call of an eagle, this was Heaven on Earth. I would stand motionless for hours at a time, just waiting and watching. If nothing else, it was a deeply relaxing endeavor where I got some of my best thinking done. After standing still for an extended period, the living landscape seemed to accept me as another piece of it. Business would go back to usual around me. River otters would pass me within a rod's length; ermines, which look like ferrets, would mischievously work down the bank, and an occasional brown bear would make an appearance, too. But the arrival of a formation of reds is what I waited for. I don't know the particular nomenclature for the part of my brain that becomes energized when this happens, but some synapses definitely spark and I can tell you that the feeling never got old.

These fish, each having spent several years deep in the North Pacific, now found themselves in a completely new environment. It seemed difficult for them to determine friend from foe, with the latter usually being associated with rapid movements. A slow and deliberate cast was the goal as I unhurriedly sidestepped up the river to keep pace. Schools ranged from pairs of fish to groupings over fifty. Larger schools of fish actually made it more difficult at times, as there was no one target to present to, you just put it in the center mass and hoped one of them saw it and responded before it was accidently caught on another's dorsal fin. In knee-deep water, watching the fly disappear and seeing the salmon begin to shake its head back and forth was the sure sign of success. Being confined to essentially a two-dimensional river, the runs and acrobatics were impressive. All you could do was keep the rod tip up as the fish ran, and then eventually run after in waders.

Although I have landed several hundred of these beautiful fish on my fly rod, my first red stands out. I was fresh to Kodiak and with the run rapidly winding down, I was hoping to hook one of these ghosts. The tide was flooding in the river that day, which was decreasing the downstream flow of the river itself to the point that it would begin flowing backward. I was on the far side and had to head back soon or else I would be in over my waders. As I stood there, I watched a single, big red come up the river. Although the water was relatively deep, I casted my chartreuse fly upstream of the fish and followed the drift with my rod tip. The next thing I remember was the fish exploding out of the water with my fly in the corner of its mouth. All I wanted to do was land this fish, but it seemed to have other plans, as it would race downstream and then turn around and blast up, throwing itself out of the water in the process. Running on loose rocks in waders with an arched over rod must have been fun to watch, if I wasn't the one doing it. Regardless, I was able to tire out the fish and slide him into the shallows. I still recall the satisfaction later that evening of placing three bags of salmon on my otherwise completely empty freezer shelves. I knew it was the start of something beautiful.

They are the first of the salmon to arrive each season in Kodiak. After months of patiently riding out winter storms and cold days, the arrival of the reds is what truly signals the beginning of summer. I would be in the river weeks before their anticipated arrival, scouting, patiently watching and hoping to see the first. Each day was different than the previous when it came to reds. A combination of tides, rain, water levels, seals, and other unknowns would cause highs and lows. But I knew that as soon as Memorial Day had passed, I would be working the rivers for reds.

Fishing Log: 24 July

Two reds, Hayden got two. Epic. Got them an hour after low tide up to an 8.2-foot-high tide, overcast. Great day!

My brother-in-law, Hayden, had come up to stay a week and do some fishing. We had been picking away at the fish, but the rivers were not on fire. The tides were weak and the rains had not fallen enough to raise the river levels to sufficiently draw in a lot of fish. Planning a trip to Alaska can be tough; after all the work that goes into it, a lack of rain the week before can make or break the whole thing. This was Hayden's last day and his last shot at really having a great trip. After wrapping up work, we had planned to start fishing at low tide to see if anything would come in as it rose. It was forecasted to be a large tide and salmon have a habit of riding that influx of water up the river. Likewise, the weather had changed; the warm sunny days had given way to overcast skies and the threat of rain. This was salmon weather and we had a good feeling. We got to the spot by midafternoon and started scouting.

Unlike other forms of salmon fishing, with reds, you did more looking than casting. If you didn't see fish moving, it was usually not worth putting a line in. It seems every time I would blindly cast, that would be the moment that a surge of fish would appear, and I would not be set up to make a good presentation of my fly. So, we walked along the river quietly, looking and waiting. As the tide began to flood, the fish showed up—in big numbers. First, they were singles or doubles, then they just poured in, big schools of twenty-plus fish, large specimens coming up the river. We had the place to ourselves and we were having a great time. These brutes were waiting to move upstream, and the surge of the tide was enough to get them going. Our flies were not welcomed and when hooked, they went wild. With the limit being two a piece, we filled our quotas in short order and watched the schools of fish continue to move upriver. These were some of the consistently biggest reds I had seen in my time on the island and I wanted to memorialize the fish beyond a photo.

Called *Gyotaku* in Japan, it is the process of making a mount of a fish by covering it in ink and rolling it onto rice paper. Before photos, this was the most accurate way of remembering a fish. There is no exaggerating sizes or camera trickery with a fish print. While fish can now be mounted, there is something special in having the exact print of the fish that was caught. Each scar, missing scale, and uniqueness of that particular fish is brought out on the paper. In Hawaii, this art form has made a big resurgence due to a renowned local artist and friend of ours, Naoki Hayashi. While nowhere close to being at his skill level, these fish seemed like good ones to practice on.

When I brought the fish back that day, I coated two of the larger specimens in an accurate design of blue, silver, and black, capturing all the details of their coloration. Gently covering the fish in the paper and pressing it along the body, the result was a perfect reflection of the fish. Using water soluble ink, I was able to completely wash off the ink from the fish, which was then filleted and later consumed. Long gone, the memory of that day and those fish hang proudly on my wall; those tanker prints now remind me of the day when perseverance paid off.

The reds continued through June and July before tapering off in August, as the next species of salmon took over the river system. Reds usually spawn in a terminal lake and will remain in their natal lake through the summer, transitioning from chrome silver to bright red. By late summer the bright fish, looking like giant goldfish, stand out in the lake. They soon die after spawning and sink to the bottom, providing food for the next generation of reds to begin their journey.

They are smaller than all other salmon varieties, except the pink salmon, and arrive early in the season when the weather can still be cold, but they are my favorite. Compact, spirited, and phenomenal to eat, to see them begin their annual march up the river reminds me that another season has begun. In many other parts of the country they no longer make this journey, being victims of habitat destruction, dams, and pollution. But to see wild fish complete their annual journey like they have for a millennium is a special feeling. Up here, their cycle is completed year after year and that is something that will never be taken for granted by me.

My dad and I made the trip back to Kodiak recently in the summer, purposefully earlier than in other years in order to catch the red run. Arriving a day before he did, I quickly shook my gear down after getting off the plane, donned my chest waders, and jumped into a river. I had taken the red-eye flight and had been too excited to sleep. I was exhausted, but did not want to waste precious fishing time by sleeping. I had come up to see the reds, my old friends. The trees were still not fully in bloom and the cold air temperatures likewise made it feel like summer had yet to begin. But based on my previous years' records, I knew the reds had to be running. I moved as fast as I could to the river to see if they were in yet.

Red fishing is often a game of patience, and I was prepared to make a day out of it if I had to. I hadn't been in the water for more than twenty minutes before I saw what looked like a formation of apparitions marching up the river toward their mortal fate. There is a moment when you see these gray ghosts, which causes you to lock up with excitement. Luckily, I got a cast off in relatively short order and hooked one. The euphoria of tangling with my first red in a few years made me laugh out loud; I had missed these fish. The salmon quickly blasted downstream and took me well into the backing of my line fast. I landed it one hundred yards down from where I hooked it. After a great fight, I guided him into the shallows and slid my hand underneath its belly. I thanked that first fish and let it swim away.

Silvers Are Pure Gold

Kings own my dreams, reds have domain of my freezer, but silvers most often have my attention. Surpassed by only kings and chums in size, silvers are a relatively large Pacific salmon species and represent the entire package: big, hard fighting, and tasty, and they will chase down lures with reckless abandon. My biggest was probably close to eighteen pounds, caught with a fly rod in a small stream. To constrain a fish this big in a river so small was the literal representation of a bull in a china shop. Silver salmon begin their annual freshwater migration in August, right as the peak of the pink salmon run has passed, and continue well into October. I have even ventured out in early January to catch spawned out silvers who had long deposited their eggs or milt and were waiting for death.

While kings require deep, fast rivers in which to spawn, and reds usually require those rivers that begin with a lake, silvers have less stringent requirements and will therefore travel up a greater number of river systems. They are the exclamation point to the end of summer and arrive at a time when many fishermen have correctly loaded out their freezers and smokers with the fish they need for the months ahead. Silvers are a celebration of the end of the season. Their arrival begins with lush green mountains and ends with the stark reality that winter is about to arrive.

By early fall, most Alaskans are overwhelmed with the choices that are available to them. On the land, hunting season is in full swing, with big game hunts ranging from moose to deer going on. In the ocean, kings and halibut are still available and feeding heavily for those willing to fish the increasingly smaller weather windows. In the rivers, the silvers begin to flood in. All this creates a sense of urgency for Alaskans. With most freezers looking well supplied with fish but light on meat, hunting is an easy choice. This becomes more apparent as September gives way to October, with its terminal snow on the mountaintops and rapidly decreasing daylight. But for those willing to resist the urge to put down the rod and pick up a rifle, early October is the time when the tankers come in.

My brother-in-law, Hayden, and his friend Ondrej were our first visitors to Kodiak, six weeks after our wedding. Arriving in early October, it was a last-minute trip. Neither had been to Kodiak but had heard enough of my stories from the summer to be intrigued. They arrived with fly rods in hand and were ready to fish. Any long-range trip to chase salmon is a gamble. Closely tied to the amount of rainfall, arriving during either a dry period, or conversely a time of heavy rains, can have a dramatic effect on success rates. Salmon will begin to school outside of their natal rivers for several weeks but do not immediately charge the river to begin their journey. Rather, they either use the incoming tide or more often an increase in river flow as a sign to make their ascent. Hayden and Ondrej's arrival was unique for several reasons. First, they arrived during a full moon, which caused a ten-foot tide. I remember the tide rising so high that I saw a seal swimming in the river nearly a half mile from the ocean. Secondly, their timing corresponded with a large rainfall on the second day. The intensity and duration of rain in Kodiak is something that is found in few other places. It once rained twenty-four hours a day for eight days straight while I was living there. That second day after their arrival was something for the books. Prior to their visit, the weather was rather dry, meaning that there was likely a backlog of silvers waiting for the rivers to rise. Fishing on the third day was challenging. The tremendous rain was just beginning to taper off, but the rivers where all high, off-color, and swift. We casted brightly colored weighted flies, known as the "chuck and duck" method, as the big flies would strike you in the back of the head from time to time. We had a few follow-ups but the river was just blown out and it was tough to do much in those conditions.

The fourth day brought clear, calm skies. The storm had moved out, and the rivers were all doing their best to shed the millions of gallons that had fallen over the last several days. We again went down to fish and see if this was going to be our day. The sun was shining, but the river still carried the wounds from the storm. Working up and down through most of the morning, we had no luck, the water was still too swollen to get the flies down without them being swept away. It didn't stop us from trying, however. The tough conditions and overlap with deer season motivated other would-be fishermen that day to focus their attention elsewhere, resulting in the three of us having the river to ourselves for the final three days of the visit. We took a break on the bank for lunch and just watched. The river was clearing up and the water level was beginning to drop. Looking back, that moment, the first initial drop of the river level, proved to be my best time for salmon. It signaled a green light for those fish waiting just outside the mouth of the river that this was the time when the bears, seals, and eagles would have the hardest time catching them.

Ondrej saw them first. "There are fish here!" At first, I almost couldn't believe it, having worked the river all morning without seeing too many signs of life, but he was right. We began to visibly see schools of fish moving up the river—one, two, then ten at a time. The slightly off-color water and surface turbulence concealed us as we began sight casting to massive salmon. Having been feeding the whole time in the ocean, these fish were not only the last of the season, they were also the biggest.

A well-presented cast above the transiting fish led to a violent hookup as the fish erupted and cartwheeled down the river. It took off and showed little sign of stopping. I was running in waders through the river, trying to keep it tight. The fish settled into the next deep hole downstream as it plotted its next move. Looking into the water, I saw a solid shoal of salmon as the sun reflected off their flanks. They just kept coming. I landed my fish and placed it on the stringer, but I was stunned by the sheer volume of salmon that continued to push up the river. We stayed till late afternoon, each of us easily filling our limits as we pondered the day we just had. My fly box was severely depleted, telling a story of fish lost and monofilament leaders shredded. It was the perfect ending to the season, the exclamation point I needed to think about as I sat at my desk tying flies throughout the long and dark winter.

Following silver seasons did not disappoint either, even though each season was different than the previous due to the weather. During low water seasons, the silvers were located at the mouths of the rivers, cautiously entering mainly on high tides. Other seasons, when the rains did not abate and the rivers were over their banks and the color of coffee, the fish transited freely upstream without interruption from humans, bears, or eagles. Additionally, the high, cold, and well-oxygenated water excited the silvers. They abandoned their low water prudence and instead behaved as if they had a chip on their shoulders. Unlike reds, which were in a hurry to get up the river and to a lake, silvers were in less of a rush to go too far, but were rather content to hang out in deep pools while they waited for the signal to change to their spawning colors. Since I knew each bend and hole of the local rivers, this was a time when I would often put my fly rod down and pick up a spinning rod and a bag full of salmon eggs.

Silvers and also king salmon have a real affinity for eating other salmon's eggs. While most salmon are not interested in feeding upon entering freshwater, eggs were an exception. The nutrient-rich eggs of competitors were freely consumed. During a period of sustained rains, I had found a bend in the river that was stacked with big, angry silvers.

Fishing Log: 26 August

Two silvers. Weather was rainy and overcast. River high but fishable, 0600-0700 in the eddy, on eggs. One fish was big!

The daily limit of silvers was two per day. During the late summer and fall, I would often wake up before work to hit some local rivers for an hour before getting in. If things went as planned, I would have two fresh silvers on ice before most people had their morning coffee. This particular fall, the late summer rains came in heavy. Kodiak does most things to the extreme, whether that be bears, mountains, or in this case, rain. With the recent large storms, the rains came in at full force, and the rivers rose fast. This first big rain washed out all the zombie pink salmon and was the green light that the oceanic silvers were awaiting, signaling them to go. The elevated water levels also spread the fish out throughout the river systems so they could be found miles upstream as well as at the mouth. I was drawn to one deep hole that I felt certain would be loaded with fish, the perfect spot for them to sit and catch their breath. Like most things in life, timing is everything. During this season, the fish seemed to want to bite mostly at first light, what mariners would call "nautical twilight," when the first signs of the sun would appear in the east. Due to Kodiak's latitude and the time of the year, the days were rapidly getting shorter and this twilight window lasted longer than normal, as the sun begrudgingly rose each day.

Crossing the high, swollen river in the dark was not my favorite part. The normally shallow gravel bar crossing that typically didn't come up past my calves was now up to my hip. This made walking across it in the dark a tricky situation, as one misstep and I was going for a ride downstream. But the spot to fish was on the far side of the river and could not be properly fished from anywhere else, so I marched on.

After safely reaching the far side I set up my rig with the aid of a headlamp. A glob of fresh neon-red eggs from a previously caught silver was the ideal bait, and I gingerly lobbed it out to the current line that separated the calm backwater eddy from the raging river. Knowing that the light from my headlamp would spook any fish sitting nearby, all the casts and retrieves had to be done in the dark, just based on feeling. A strike on eggs is not like most other hits. It feels softer, less like a hammer and more like a fish chewing a mouth full of jelly beans. The key is not to rip the hook back; rather, just slowly reel.

As I came tight on the fish, the surface of the roiling river exploded. The strong currents were providing heavy torque on the size-four hook. I had given the fish ample time to ingest the bait, and I was hoping that it was firmly in the corner of its jaw. Taking flight numerous times, the pool didn't provide enough runway for the fish to get airborne, so it took off downstream. Combined with the river's speed, it moved like a torpedo, until I was able to turn its head and start working it toward the shore while I made haste down the river after it. Every salmon has this unique roll/flop it does before it is landed. Best described as a gator-roll, the multi-axis escape routine has freed many a fish back to the river as the hook cannot hold. Luckily, the hook held enough this time as I ran it up onto the flooded grass shoreline. It was a big male and a fish to be proud of. Even luckier, a few casts later and I was tight with a second fish.

Pinks and Chums

The downside of living in Alaska is that you become a salmon snob. Fish that I would once have gladly kept and eaten gradually seem beneath one's station. Even bears feel this way. Early in the season, bears will consume as much of a salmon as they can. By late summer, I watch them catch a pink salmon, eat only the belly meat and eggs, and leave the rest for the eagles

and magpies. The bounty of the shear biomass allows consumers, both two- and four-legged, to be choosy.

Pinks, or humpies, by individual size are the smallest
of the salmon, usually under six pounds, but in terms of
sheer volume, they are a mighty sight to behold. By July,
they begin to ascend the rivers in numbers that will make
you stop just to watch. The river turns black with the backs of
these fish swimming upstream. Hundreds of thousands
of them, migrating up seemingly any creek that they can
float in, is a sight that I thought was limited to National
Geographic documentaries. For new fishermen or just for
those of us who want to have a good day fishing, they are
a blast to catch.

If there was ever a fish to teach a child how to fish on, a
pink salmon is it. Nearly every cast can result in a hook-up and
spirited fight. The downside of the pinks is that by the time
they reach the river, they are beginning to change from their
oceanic chrome-silver coloration to a muted, splotchy brown/
white/olive-green hue. This quick transition to its spawning
colors indicates that the fish's metamorphosis has begun, and
it will soon consume itself in the pursuit of its life's mission
to spawn and die. The external coloration of the salmon has
a corresponding color change on the inside. The fish's flesh
becomes pale and softer during this process. The soft, pale
meat is not as appetizing, and so pinks get a bad rap when
compared to their more notable and larger cousins. Pinks
caught in the ocean are good table fare, however, they are
not terribly freezer friendly. Their fillets are more compa-
rable to trout: soft, delicate, and best served either fresh or

smoked. Someone saying a particular fish is good smoked is a bit of a red-flag to me. After all, with the right amount of sugar, salt, and hardwood smoke added, nearly anything will taste great.

Pinks begin to wear out their welcome by the time the silvers hit the river. By August, the thousands of pinks begin to resemble zombies, with their flesh falling off their bones and staggering changes to their bone structure. The males develop a large hump on their back that makes them look huge, thus the nickname humpies. These zombie fish wander throughout the river and are a bane to anglers, often taking lures and baits meant for the more prodigious silver salmon. As they begin to die, the rotting carcasses of pinks litter the riverbanks and river bottoms, stinking up the entire area. The water seems off-color with the protein shake of pink salmon matter suspended in the water. It is not until the first heavy rains come and wash all this out to sea that the river seems to be restored.

However, pink salmon feed and fertilize Alaska's animals and land. While they cannot compete bite-for-bite with the other species, they are a sight to behold and are evidence that this level of bounty still exists in the world.

Chums are the more clandestine of the species, at least on Kodiak. They get larger than all but kings and suffer the same reputation as pinks, although, anecdotally, they are the least common salmon I've ever crossed paths with. There was only one river I knew of where I could find chums with some consistency, otherwise they were just seen occasionally. Quickly changing to their spawning colors, most chums caught are not in premier palatable shape.

When caught at sea, they are good fish to eat. An emerging commercial market for chums is beginning to take hold. The word "chum" doesn't quite inspire savory thoughts, so it will often be marketed as keta salmon, taken from its scientific name *Oncorhynchus keta*. But when hooked in rivers, they are a photogenic fish to land. The purple and green patterns are distinctive and their large size make the battle exciting. They do not do the leaps of a silver, nor the sprints of a red. They are bulldogs and will use their size to resist being landed. However, most are released to continue on their journey with a photo being the best way to enjoy them.

Halibut

The antithesis of a precise fly presentation to a lone salmon is to fish for halibut. A fish with a nickname of "barn door" doesn't worry much about presentation. Halibut fishing in Alaska is wild. Ninety percent of your trip will be uneventful and the other ten percent will be about the same level as a bare-knuckle bear fight. They are big, delicious, and at times dangerous to pursue. While salmon often require a degree of finesse and psychological smarts to catch, halibut require heavier tackle, a stout stomach, and patience. Although they can reach weights of over four hundred pounds, most caught by day-boat fisherman are under fifty pounds, which are often referred to as "chickens." They are the ideal eating size. While there may be glory in landing a monster fish, I will take a smaller one for the freezer anytime. A big halibut has tougher meat than a smaller one, much like comparing an old bull to veal.

Typically, they are not fussy about line diameter nor hook size, and they do not take kindly to being winched off the bottom and placed on the deck of a boat. Tightly managed at the state, federal, and international level, halibut are one of the main economic drivers for fishing in Alaska. The key to halibut fishing is finding them, and not being in the right spots can make for a very slow day.

In June of my first summer on Kodiak, my brothers flew up for a week to experience Alaska firsthand. I had wintered over and cut my teeth on nearly a full year of fishing; I was anxious to share that knowledge with them. I had visions of putting on a clinic, piles of red salmon and carpets of halibut. What we all learned was that fish don't jump onto your hook anywhere, even in Alaska. Don't believe the brochures.

Fishing Log: 25 June

Halibut with Rory and Pat. One small chicken at buoy 3, drifting on a jig. Tried a bunch of spots—all sucked.

I have had good trips and bad trips while in Kodiak, but this was the only time I was ever out-fished. I came back to the docks and saw rookies with halibut, but we only brought back a single small halibut and a black bass, neither of which probably should have been retained in the first place. To put it simply,

I was pissed. There is nothing worse than coming up short of expectations, especially when your brothers come to visit with very high expectations.

As Josh Boyle tells me, "Always try to learn something from being in the field." I took away a few hard lessons. First, don't chase other people's intel. I went way out of my preferred area to pursue someone else's numbers. Ironically, the area I went to was essentially the most heavily fished area of Kodiak—dumb mistake. Second, be patient. I was in such a rush to put on a show that I moved before my bait could do its thing and draw in some fish. By week's end, I had one more shot at getting them on some fish before they went home with mostly empty fish boxes. It was game time.

Fishing Log: 28 June

Eight halibut to 80 lbs. including a couple of 50s. Location: Valley of the Giants, 133ft. Good incoming tide. All on bait.

I fished a spot I nicknamed "Valley of the Giants," a series of gravel hills that had yet to let me down. We got to our numbers and dropped the anchor just up current of the humps. By anchoring ahead of the spot, I could either ease the anchor out to get closer or the scent of our baits would draw the fish up to us. At first, we had no action. I knew this spot would produce if I just gave it a little time, so I patiently waited. When Rory's rod doubled over with a good fish, I breathed a sigh of relief.

The fish were here, and as he battled an estimated fifty-pound fish, I knew they both would at least be bringing some fish back home. The pressure was off.

From there we had a steady pick of forty-to-fifty-pound fish. Rory and I had caught our limits, but Pat had one fish to go. It was getting a little later in the day and it was time to start thinking about wrapping it up. Not long after, Pat's rod doubled over. Big fish seem to know which hook is attached to the smallest rod. Of course, Pat was using my lightweight salmon trolling rod, more suitable for downrigger trolling than a Pacific halibut. That Shimano Trevala rod doubled over and then some as the line came tight. Pat was in for a battle and that little Avet SX reel was earning its keep.

I can reasonably gauge the size of a halibut by the number of runs. One small run, the fish is under twenty-five pounds; two solid runs, thirty to fifty pounds; and three-plus big runs means the halibut is closer to three digits. As Pat's fish took its third big run, I knew this was a good fish. He could barely put enough pressure on the fish with the light tackle but was slowly gaining line. Knowing this was a big fish on light line, we rigged up the harpoon once again. This was the safest way of landing a larger halibut. It also prevented knife fights or having the fish go nuts once brought into the boat. It came up smooth after that third run, and Rory drilled it with the harpoon. The fish made a short run but with the harpoon line firmly attached to it, we knew we had secured its capture. With our last fish boated, we finished a fantastic trip.

None of our catch that day were giants, but we caught our limit of perfect eating-sized halibut, each one between forty and ninety pounds. Lesson learned: make your own intel. By the time you get word that a hot bite is going on, it's probably over. Be the one who makes the fishing reports, because once the sun sets, the reset button is hit. The key for halibut fishing is location. Take the time to find an area that seems productive and provides the right conditions for this ambush predator to set their trap. If you have confidence in an area, do not give up on it without investing a bit of time. Also, if you nicknamed an area the Valley of the Giants, start there.

<hr />

Fishing Log: 03 July

One 180 lb. halibut. Waypoint number 41 in 74 feet of water at Sullivan's Rocks. The tide was hauling ass. Spin-in-glo squid skirt and squid. One bite. Weather sucked, cloudy and cold.

The summer after my brothers' first visit, my neighbor Dave asked if I would take him and his son, who was visiting from South Carolina, out fishing. The weather was pretty nasty, but we decided to stick our noses out. After fishing the Valley of the Giants for a few hours in some snotty seas without any action, I was confident that they were not home and it was time to move on. Panning through the chart like a football coach looking for a fourth and one play, I found what I wanted— another raised gravel bottom spot adjacent to a rock pile that was also out of the building sea state. This spot had produced for me in the past. It was a slow bite but often a big one.

After motoring over and dropping the anchor, I explained that this spot would produce, but it was a matter of being patient and letting our baits and the current work their magic. An hour later, our patience paid off. The current picked up. Not long after, I felt the distinctive *rat tat tat* of a halibut. I gave the fish a rod's length of slack and slowly lifted up. It felt like I hooked into the drain plug of the ocean itself. It didn't give at all, and the rod came to a stop halfway up on the swing. I could tell it was a fish of consequence, and it started taking line. I handed the rod off to Dave's twenty-something son to let him feel the weight of a real halibut. I was surprised he couldn't gain ground on the fish. I was using a Penn International 12, which has a two-speed reel setting, and after watching him struggle, I leaned over and dropped the reel into low gear, the first time I needed to do that on a halibut. After a good amount of winching, a brown rug appeared off the starboard quarter. I drilled the fish as hard as I could with the harpoon, but it didn't punch through the other side; it was a thick fish. With a gaff and help, the three of us slid a barn door over the gunwale. It was a beast! We had nowhere to put it and knew it was time to head home. The awful ride back to the dock through those big seas didn't dampen our morale. Back at the dock, the fish topped out at one hundred and eighty-five pounds and remains the biggest halibut I have landed on rod and reel.

One consistent fact I have learned across all fisheries is that you don't have to go far to catch big fish. However, shore fishermen will always seek to make the farthest cast, and boat fishermen will seek to run the farthest offshore. The general belief is that the fish are always "way out there," and to be successful, you have to go as far as possible out to sea. The fish must know this, because I keep finding areas very close to the dock that hold very large fish. Having found success in Gloucester catching whale cod on inshore spots, I had a hunch that halibut might be the same.

My friend and fellow coastie Jim Morrow, aka Earthworm Jim, and I had plans to head out one late summer day to chase halibut in the Valley of the Giants. As with many North Pacific summer days, the difference between the air and ocean temperatures caused a sizable fog bank to form just off the coast. With both of us being paid in part for our ability to assess risk, we decided to forgo the offshore run and try some inshore spots, not far off the beach where the visibility was still good. We recalibrated our expectations: if we caught fish, it was a win, and if we didn't, well that's what we expected to happen, and we would chalk it up to being in the wrong location. Sometimes, though, forcing yourself to try somewhere new pays off.

Fishing Log: 25 July

Two halibut, five total at the boat. Fished with Earthworm Jim, foggy. 70 feet of water. Incoming tide, big fish was 70 lbs. Used herring. Pretty awesome.

By this point in the season, the pink salmon were in full swing and they began to ascend nearly all rivers by the thousands.

This much feed could not have gone unnoticed, so we searched and found a spot in proximity to pink salmon areas that also had some nice bottom contour changes—a place where an ambush hunter might want to lie in wait. It was so close to the beach that it seemed we should have left the boat on the shore and used pool inflatables inside. Other boats would pass us wondering if we had broken down, decided to go for a swim, or were just clueless. We watched people walking down the shore with their dogs looking at us. Dropping the anchor, we sat waiting for the scent of our baits to work their magic. Sure enough, an hour later, Jim took a strike and landed a great looking halibut in the seventy-pound range. This was awesome. It was not a monster, but with the size of a pink salmon, I had a hunch larger halibut were in the area. We were onto something, and more research was needed.

Fishing Log: 27 July

One 135 lb. halibut, plus a 65 lb. and 90 lb. with Father John. Fished all day in 78 feet of water. Sunny and hot, moving tide is needed. Dropped two big fish as well.

I returned to try it out during a local fishing tournament I had organized through work—no prizes or money, just for bragging rights and maybe a homemade trophy. But I had a reputation to uphold. The weather was unusually beautiful on this Friday in August as we all set off in our various boats to ply the waters for halibut. Resisting the urge to run miles off to undiscovered rocky pinnacles, I brought the boat instead to my new inshore spot. Perched alongside coastal hikers and dog walkers, it looked more like a fishing spot you would choose if you were afraid of the water, rather than a spot for a trophy hunter. It was a place where you could walk back ashore if things went sideways. My rod doubling over changed that thought rather quickly. Being so shallow, the large halibut was forced to run horizontal instead of vertical, and I laughed with excitement as line peeled off my reel. On this trip I took with me my friend and local priest, Father John. He had heard stories of Alaska's big halibut and wanted to experience it firsthand. Perhaps he brought with him a little divine intervention as well. The big fish exhausted itself on its initial runs and it came to the surface vertically, making harpooning it more of a challenge. But with a side-ways thrust, the bronze dart passed through the fish and locked itself against the other side. It was not getting away now, despite one more adrenaline-fueled sprint. The fish was big, weighing in at one hundred and thirty-five pounds.

The lines went back down, and it didn't take long for the rod to once again double over. After another valiant fight, we landed a ninety-pound fish. Soon after, a sixty-five-pounder joined the cooler. Despite not filling our limits, we had more than enough fish to fill the freezer and also had a fair amount of work ahead of us in processing, so we decided to call it a trip. The weigh-in station was pretty quiet when I hoisted the larger halibut onto the scales, beating its nearest competitor, our other fish, by forty-five pounds.

Either big fish know where the boat ramp is and hide there to avoid being caught by anglers hell bent on getting way out there, or, more likely, there is no correlation between distance traveled and fish caught. Moral of the story: fish local.

The Ayakulik

To the rest of the world, Alaska is remote. To Alaskans, Kodiak is remote, reserved for fishermen, coastguardsmen, and brown bears. But to the residents of Kodiak, the "off the road system" is remote. And if you were going to pick the farthest corner of off the road system, you would find the Ayakulik River. Seventy-five miles from the town of Kodiak, and a million miles from society, the Ayakulik is one of Kodiak's two rivers that proudly boast a natural run of king salmon. Located among the Kodiak National Wildlife Refuge and native Alaskan land, the closest full-time human population is the village of Karluk, which is located along the Shelikof Strait. This village holds a special place in my heart, as Renee used to work here, taking a small bush plane into the village once a month to work with the village's two full-time teachers, who also happen to be the nicest of people.

There are only two manmade structures near the Ayakulik. They are small cabins run by Ayakulik Adventures. I lucked out on this trip by bidding on it at a local charity auction one winter's night. I was over the moon to have scored such a prize and started planning for it immediately. The hardest part was finding someone who wanted to go with me. My brothers and dad could not make it, and all my usual fishing buddies had legitimate reasons for not being able to come along. So, I went on the five-day trip alone.

Getting there was no easy task. Your options are an overnight boat ride, a dicey float plane ride, or a helicopter. You guessed it: the trip included the helicopter ride. It was in early June that I set out. The fog was thick that Monday and I expected that the flight was a no-go. But as a former Coast Guard pilot, Tom had no issues with it. We took off and hugged the ground within fifty feet for much of the trip. It was as exhilarating as a roller-coaster ride as we skimmed the hilltops and water. Seventy-five miles and a step back in time and we were there.

We arrived as the week's prior guests, who were the first fishing clients of the season, were departing. For five days they plied the waters without seeing a fish. Then, the day before I arrived, the salmon showed up—with a name like Conor Sullivan, we agreed it had to be the luck of Irish.

Fishing Log: 13 June

Ayakulik. 40,000 sockeye came through the weir today. I must have caught at least twenty fish. I have never seen so much fish and as the jacked up Alaska Department of Fish and Game (ADF&G) kid said, "I was a part of it." The lodge is awesome—simple, quiet, and surrounded by fish. I only wish I had a brother or my dad with me to share it. This is a place to do some thinking and to awaken what is important in me. I may never find such a pure place. I am not sure what the future holds for me, but I know I need to be con-nected to the water and earth; it is who I am. It's midnight and I am writing this with my headlamp. Time to rack out and tomorrow, live the dream. I have the Eddie Vedder soundtrack for Into the Wild *playing through my head. I can't help it.*

It was the only time in my life I got bored catching reds. Back in town, I would dedicate hours to seeing a single red salmon. Here, I watched thousands come by in one afternoon. Most casts hooked one, and a five fish limit was easy to reach. The reds were a sight to see, all hugging the shoreline, making their way up like an unbroken teal-blue line. What I was really after, though, were the wild kings. While the reds numbered in the thousands, the kings were just in the hundreds. Wild kings statewide had had some tough years recently, and here in the Ayakulik it was no different. For unknown reasons, king salmon numbers had been historically low. There were numerous theories as to why, but the facts were that there were just not a lot of kings returning. I had to temper my expectations of hooking into a wild king on a fly rod. I had a week to do it and, despite all the reports, I had a feeling I could pull it off.

The second night I had my first contact with one. While drifting a small fly meant for reds in the fastest, deepest section of the river toward the mouth, I snagged what I thought was the bottom. As I stepped out into the river to free my fly, the "snag" slowly moved away. The fish seemed not bothered by my nine-weight rod pulling it—never running, but not relenting either. After a sluggish tug-of-war, I slid the fifteen-pound chrome-bright fish into the shallows to unhook and release it. It was foul-hooked, which explained the unusual fight. This fish was big, wild, and focused on getting back to the business of swimming upstream. It was proof that the big kings were in, I just had to keeping working for them. I learned right away that I was not the only one interested in landing salmon, and I was continually watching my back for one of the best fishermen out there, the Kodiak brown bear.

Second to only the polar bear, the Kodiak brown bear is about the largest bear on the planet. Biologically speaking, they are different from their mainland counterparts. Kodiak was once attached to mainland Alaska, but separated thousands of years ago. As Kodiak drifted farther away from the Alaskan Peninsula, the brown bears that remained on the island became distinct from their mainland relatives. Part of that genetic code makes them consistently huge. Additionally, the easier winters and abundance of food provides the correct environmental conditions to pack the pounds on. The best way to describe the experience of being near one is that it doesn't seem real. How can something that big actually still exist? Unlike the inland grizzly, coastal brown bears (bears within one hundred miles of the coast) are generally less aggressive toward humans, although you don't want to test the theory. When fishing on Kodiak, being aware of bears is part of deal. Both bears and humans often favor the same spots, and it is routine to see bears along the rivers while fishing. With plenty of food available, the bears and the humans can get along, but be careful if you have a fish on the line. A bear looking for an easy meal will opt to take your fish rather than grab one themselves. The patterned behavior of bears knowing that they can steal a fisherman's catch is dangerous, mostly for the bear. A bluff charge is usually all it takes to convince a fisherman to drop a fish. But bears who pattern this behavior are often the ones shot in defense of life or property. So, the game Alaskans play is like bluffing in a high-stakes poker game: act like you can win and hope the other guy doesn't call you on it. Yelling, waving your arms, and even throwing rocks are all acceptable deterrents. A gun is the last resort, reserved for moments where the person can clearly articulate that shooting the animal was justifiable in the defense of their or someone else's life. I came across plenty of bears on this trip, seeing them nearly every day. Give them space, treat them with respect, and know when to walk away.

Upon landing, I immediately saw a bear walking down the river smelling the water. After walking and sniffing, it plunged its body into the river and pulled out a dead red salmon. The water was high and off-color so there was no way the bear could have seen that fish; it somehow smelled it from the surface. These were impressive animals. The bears of the Ayakulik reminded me of giant dogs. You could tell by their body language that they were there for the fish and didn't seem to care about the human company for the most part. After a few days, the bears became recognizable. They were around every day, and while we always kept an eye on them, it was clear that for the most part they were just looking to fish as well. There was one moment while I watched a sow (female) bear and her cub chase salmon up the river that I got myself into a bit of jam. The two bears were a few hundred yards downstream of me and I was mesmerized as mama bear pounced on a salmon with the cub in tow. It was so cool to watch that I went ahead and pulled out my video camera to document it all. They were steadily making their way upstream toward me, laser-focused on the school of fish they were pursuing. All of a sudden, their pace picked up and they were hot on the tails of a school of salmon along the bank, which was directly downstream of me. I quickly went from leisurely sitting on the bank smiling with my camera one moment to up on my feet in survival mode, yelling at mama bear as she closed within ten yards of me, trying to get them to stop and see me before it was too late. The video goes from tranquil to *Blair Witch Project* pretty fast. She did realize how close I was and stopped, looked at me, and made her way back down the bank.

On the following day after a riverside lunch, I rested my rod on a willow branch and pulled my hat over my face. Listening to the river gurgle past me as my lunch warmed me from the inside was the perfect recipe for an easy nap, and I dozed off. I had been up early and fishing late each day, and it was starting to catch up with me. How much time had passed I wasn't entirely sure, but I sat up sensing something near me. Staring back at me across the river was a small herd of reindeer. Kodiak has a resident population of these on the south side, but I had never seen them until that moment. They had about the same reaction that I did, a combination of amazement, curiosity, and surprise. Not liking what they saw, they quickly trotted over the treeless tundra. To be in a place where your alarm clock can be reindeer stuck with me.

The river was off-color and swollen that week. I never got to see any kings migrating upstream, and the amount of water made it tough to work a fly. Most days were filled with swinging heavy marabou flies with sink-tip lines through the deep holes. Conditions were tough but I was undeterred. I finally connected midweek on a fish that I had been waiting for.

———

Fishing Log: 17 June

Overcast and cool, no wind, little to no rain. 30lb. king in the horseshoe hole on a black and blue fly, similar to a woolly bugger. One strike all day. One other king landed, plus rolled a couple. Nice hike up the river, the lack of trees is pretty crazy. I am still really enjoying myself and all that is out here. I cringe thinking about going back to work, emails, and bosses. I prefer the companionship of the bears and eagles. How I ever get back to a place like this, I am not sure, but I will. The ocean is still the last frontier and the Coast Guard keeps me on it.

That king today was impressive. Felt like a river tuna. The fight could have been sexier, but a fish of that size does not belong in a little river. It is a fish of 10,000 casts but it was awesome hooking one. Two more full days here—got to enjoy them.

After working a particular hole for an hour, I felt what I had been waiting for—the sudden and violent strike of a fish that did not like this intruder fly swinging past it. It was a bulldog fight, never racing down the river like a red, or jumping clear out of the water like a silver, but trying to beat me by staying deep and putting her shoulders into the current. The way the rod slammed up and down felt a lot like snagging the propeller of a boat. My knees were shaking, and I knew this was the one I had been waiting for. The nine-weight rod was in a full parabolic arch as the fish stayed deep and shook her head with displeasure. After moving up the hole and finding no relief, she came back down, the whole time not moving off the bottom. I kept thinking of what unknown snags existed deep in this hole as I tried to be perfect during this fight: rod tip up, constant pressure, and responsive to what the fish wanted to do. Finally, I was able to get her head turned and lift her out of the depths. Slowly backpedaling to keep constant pressure, she finally abated and came into the shallows. A wild Kodiak king on a fly—it was a proud moment. Being a resident, I could have harvested the fish, but each king counted in the Ayakulik so I eased her into the current and let her go, off to complete her journey.

My week on the Ayakulik went by fast. Returning, it felt like I now lived in New York City, as the low hum of the town now seemed busy. A simple life exists out there, if you are willing to sacrifice for it. That week on the Ayakulik was the best recharge for the soul I had ever found. It proved how simple life and how peaceful standing thigh-deep in a river all day can be. The sheer mass of reds migrating upstream was impressive, and the power of the kings was humbling, but what I did not expect was how the wildlife, and particularly the bears, would be the most amazing.

My quest for red salmon continued. I had been invited to fish a river on Kodiak that was only accessible with an all-terrain vehicle (ATV). It wasn't the Ayakulik, but it was one hell of a day trip. Back in town, I might fish an entire day to catch my limit of two salmon, but out there, the limit was five, and I came close to catching that in as many casts. After that first trip with my buddy Dave, I was on a mission to find an ATV. It was the first time a fishing trip motivated me to buy a vehicle. The sad day that Josh Boyle had to leave the island, bound for Cordova, was also the day Renee and I picked up our side-by-side ATV. It looked like a mini pickup truck and was our ticket to the river. Wearing our new dirt bike helmets, we set off early one June morning for our inaugural run with a few friends.

Fishing Log: 16 July

Five for me, three for Renee. Sunny and hot. Started fishing at 0700. Bears—buy a gun. Fish all under the overhanging branches.

Just getting there was an adventure. The trail started easy. It was a dirt road that led to a number of creek crossings, each one bringing water up to the floorboards or higher, necessitating that waders be worn for the transit. Then it was time to start our ascent up the trail. The knobby tires of the side-by-side were straining for traction as we kept working up the ruts in the trail. When we reached the mountain pass, an area that is sometimes snowbound until May, we took a quick stretch break without shutting down the machine, for fear that it wouldn't turn back on. Back in the ATV, it was time for the sketchy part of the journey: a half-mile stretch of basketball- to television-sized jagged rocks. The key to not shredding tires is to try not to steer. Rather, let the wheels go where they want. After navigating our way through this level, it was on to some dusty straightaways, followed by a series of large puddle/small pond crossings. Each one is a gamble, as many a rider has chosen poorly and had their vehicle completely submerged. This happened to me once. I chose wrong and had to scramble out the front window before my machine tipped over. If you made it through all this, without getting lost at the end from the numerous trail options, you were greeted by a river that contained some of the best fishing I have ever encountered.

On our first run, Renee and I were doing well until the boulder field got us. It wasn't long after we cleared it that I realized we had a large gash in our front left tire. I did have a spare, but no jack. Being sixteen miles out in the Alaska bush from the closest tire shop, it was time to get creative. With help, we used the winch on the front bumper to connect to a large tree branch and lift the front end off the ground, enough to slide a log under. With the front propped up, we changed the tire and made it to the river.

Just as I expected, our early arrival yielded no other fishermen, but plenty of salmon. There was a slight bend in the river that created a depression in the bottom. This was my favorite spot. Even without polarized sunglasses, a large, stationary formation of teal was plainly visible, representing numerous large salmon, stacked on each other like cord wood.

Armed with our fly rods, we would cast well ahead of the school and drift our flies through.

Nearly every cast resulted in a hook-up. Upon taking the fly, the fish would open its mouth and violently shake its head, attempting to rid itself of this unknown force. If the hook held, it would either shoot up- or downstream like a rocket, with speeds so fast that you wondered if you were going to get spooled. If the hook and the leader still held, then the salmon would come out of the water on multiple backflips, all the while shaking its head. Pull too hard at this moment and the leader will break; induce too much slack and the hook will fly free. As you regained line and could feel victory at hand, the salmon would do it all over again. It typically took three good runs for the fish to use up its energy stores enough to be beached. Nets aren't typically used on Kodiak, so we would backpedal and have the salmon ground itself on the shore.

Fishing was hot that morning, and we all were having success. By nine, I had limited out and Renee had a few more to go. I was watching her battle her next fish, and she was getting the hang of when to let it run and when to take in line. Her salmon was on its last run and heading begrudgingly toward the shore. As Renee backed up against the thick alders that lined that bank, the trees came alive, shaking violently as the distinct roar of a Kodiak brown bear let us know our morning was about to change.

I felt myself roll back in time several thousand years as I saw the bear lunge out of the alders toward Renee. It was aggressively huffing, loudly exhaling, and looking to move us off our pile of salmon. Dave and I quickly positioned ourselves between Renee and the bear. It was about fifteen feet from us. Dave drew his large caliber revolver from his chest holster, and the three of us stared at each other, hearing only our pounding hearts—or was it each other's? While it lasted only a few seconds, being that close to something that enormous and wild made the moment seem like forever. We didn't budge, nor did the bear. It expected us to scoot out of there and seemed to be trying to figure out its next move as we stared at it and each other. The revolver could not compete with a thousand pounds of muscle, and, frankly, we could maybe have gotten off one shot before one of us was toast. We shouted and yelled at it, although I don't remember what we said. Thankfully, the bear's attitude changed as we stood our ground. With a snort that I interpreted as a brown bear obscenity, it withdrew into the brush, never to been seen again that day. Renee walked over to me, and I recall as clear as day what she said: "You need to buy a big gun when we get home."

Of all my trips into the mountains and rivers of Kodiak, this was my most intense bear encounter. I had others, like the time I had one lumber in behind me while fishing in the dark, but none of them were as aggressive as this one. Unlike the bears on the Ayakulik, this one must have previously found success bluff charging fishermen and taking their catch. To give in was to reward bad behavior, which would unfortunately end in the demise of the bear eventually. To stand your ground was a roll of the dice. It was not the typical Saturday for a newlywed couple, but then again, we weren't typical.

ABOVE: The bears of the Ayakulik River with commercial salmon boats awaiting the start of a red salmon opener. BELOW: From left to right: Conor, Patrick, and Rory Sullivan with limits of red salmon following a backcountry run.

ABOVE: Patrick Sullivan with his monster fifty-pound cod caught in vicinity of Gloucester, MA. BELOW: Trolling in paradise, heading out to the grounds on the *Ohana o Kai* with Diamond Head and Honolulu in the background.

Patrick, Conor, and Tim Sullivan with their 611-pound marlin being hoisted at Kewalo Basin.

The author's father, Tim Sullivan, with a large sunrise cod caught from the secret spot.

The author with his biggest cod to date, an estimated forty pounds.

ABOVE: The author with his sunrise surf casting catch, a forty-inch striper. BELOW: The aftermath of the knife fight with the tuna. Note the outline of the fish in the blood.

ABOVE: The author with a 180-pound halibut. BELOW LEFT: Josh Boyle and the author's mom Teresa with her first halibut. BELOW RIGHT: Renee and Conor with Renee's likely first halibut.

ABOVE: The author, his son Brayden, and daughter Anabelle with his marlin. LEFT: The tail of a 611-pound marlin.

ABOVE: Tim Sullivan with a fine looking silver salmon caught in low water conditions in early fall. BELOW: Pat Murphy and Conor with a live bait-trolled marlin.

Conor stand-up fighting a marlin.

ABOVE: A rare picture of a brown bear fishing in the surf. BELOW: A brown bear chasing salmon at the mouth of the Ayakulik River.

ABOVE: A 611-pound marlin in the bed of a friend's truck being dropped off at the auction block. BELOW: Conor and his newborn daughter Anabelle and freshly caught red salmon.

ABOVE: There is no easy way to hoist a large halibut.

LEFT: Conor and Brooks encountering a brown bear in their salmon spot.

ABOVE: Renee with a bright pink salmon. BELOW: Brother-in-law Hayden and sister Maureen shortly before her first fly rod-caught pink salmon on Kodiak.

ABOVE: From left to right: Patrick, Conor, and Rory with a bluefish caught in 1994.
BELOW: Conor hoisting what is likely his first mahi-mahi on the *Mallow*.

ABOVE: Tuna, ono, and mahi-mahi with a young Conor.
LEFT: Mike Sakamoto and Conor at a Mike Sakamoto look-alike contest.

ABOVE: The marlin stretched nearly the entire length of the *Ohana o Kai*. BELOW: Conor with son, Brayden, and one of his first fish caught in Kaneohe, HI.

ABOVE: The wild waters of Hawaii from the stern of the *Ohana o Kai*. BELOW: A brown bear on the Ayakulik River getting a better look for migrating salmon.

The author with a wild Ayakulik River king salmon.

Patrick Sullivan with his big mahi-mahi.

Renee shows the youngest, Will, how to catch stripers in Portsmouth, New Hampshire.

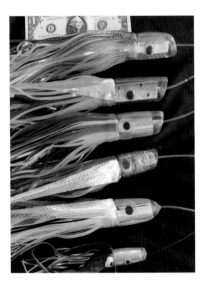 

ABOVE LEFT: A line up of homemade resin head trolling lures made by the author. ABOVE RIGHT: Conor with his birthday present spearfish off Waianae. BELOW: A battered pencil popper eye-to-eye with a hard-earned keeper striper.

ABOVE: Fishing vessel *Sea Hawk* relieving a grateful *Ohana o Kai* of a slow side tow and hauling back to shore the 611-pound marlin for Conor, Patrick, and Tim. BELOW: Rory and Patrick taking a swim call in 3,000 feet of water off the Waianae coast.

ABOVE: The great Brooks Horan heading out for a day of halibut fishing. LEFT: Jon Dale and Conor after a good morning of striper fishing with a few other friends off Rhode Island.

This river continued to produce for me. From mid-June and through July, I would be along its banks, exploring the runs and pools it had to offer. We usually made each trip with a few other friends, but nothing beats fishing with family. When my brothers decided to come up the following summer for my thirtieth birthday, I couldn't wait to show them the place. On top of that, my cousin Jake, a Coast Guard helicopter pilot, had been stationed on Kodiak that summer, too. Jake purchased a 1970s era Toyota Land Cruiser to make the trip to the river as well. The four of us trailered our rigs out to the head of the trail at 4 A.M. one morning, because to get there early was everything. The fish, under the cover of semidarkness, would push up the river all night.

———

Fishing Log: 29 June

Five reds. Rory and Pat got five as well. Not a ton of fish, 0900-1200. Great day.

Although night only lasts for minutes at that time of year, the low light and lack of pressure made the fish relaxed in the early morning hours. I liked to be already heading home by the time the rest of the fleet was just driving out.

The ride out on the trail was epic. It was a still and bright morning, the kind where each inhale renewed your soul with the smell of fireweed and alders. Our machines broke the stillness of the morning. We laughed as we forged the deep creeks and exhaled satisfactorily upon safely crossing the boulder field.

We set up in the run where Renee and I liked to fish, and the four of us had one of my most memorable days of fishing. There was a constant swoosh of a fly through the air as four archers dropped their size six flies into the drift pattern. It seemed someone's rod was always bent over with a fish. The reds were stacked, and as much as I wanted to, there was no reason to leave this spot, for there were fifty fish in an area the size of a mattress. While I had seen more fish on previous trips, we had in front of us a stationary school that was cooperative. I had limited out first, with five large salmon cooling off in the shallows. With the pressure off, I got to sit and watch my brothers fish. I left home at eighteen, and while I was gone, they had grown up and become men, and proficient fly fishermen to boot. It was nice to be together again, like when we were kids. Running from fish to fish, I played deckhand for them, landing and processing their catch.

Between the four of us, we placed twenty salmon in large coolers, each one buried in ice to maintain peak freshness and to prevent their jostling on the ride back. We made a small fire on a bluff overlooking the river, roasted a few hot dogs, and drank an obligatory Alaskan amber beer to commemorate the day. Miles from cell phone service and with not another fisherman in sight, we had found a little slice of Heaven on Earth. The bears didn't bug us on this run, which from what I could tell, was a disappointment to Rory and Pat. But it was ok with me, I had made a life long memory with my brothers, fishing the wild waters.

Fishing Log: 09 June

The last cast in Kodiak. Two reds, above Ondrej's Gate. Dad came
in and we went straight to the river. Fish were in the silver run,
deep. Landed three, beautiful weather!

I had received orders to take command of a 110-foot patrol boat
back on the East Coast, and my time on Kodiak was rapidly
coming to an end. My dad had flown up to help us pack and
had volunteered to ride down on the ferry with the car and me
from Kodiak to Bellingham, Washington, as Renee and baby
Anabelle were going to fly off the island. It was tough to say
goodbye, although I knew it was not forever. We could have
one more trip to the river if we went quickly. I swung by
the airport to meet my dad, who came in on the morning
jet. There were only two arrivals of the jet on any given day,
so this was a common way of describing one's arrival time. In
the 4Runner, I had two sets of waders and fly rods, to make
one last run on the way home. This was a risky move: Dad
had yet to meet his first granddaughter, and we knew there
could be some flak to be taken for stopping to fish. But the
river conditions were right, even if time was not on our side.
From the airport we proceeded directly to the river. Getting
our waders on at the truck felt different that day. It was a ritual
I had done hundreds of times before, but I knew this was the
last time for a while. Life was going to take me away from
Alaska for a bit and my heart ached. Geared up, we proceeded

down our trail to the river and were greeted by a spectacular June morning that was uncharacteristically Kodiak. The sun was out, the wind was low, and the air was warm. We walked into the river and immediately spotted fish moving upstream. With a quick cast we were both tight and enjoyed the moment. We beached the fish on the gravel bar as we had done dozens of times before. These fish would be harvested and shipped to me down in the lower forty-eight, allowing me to enjoy the bounty of Alaska for one more year.

Alaska is a place that gets into your soul and can have a profound impact on your life. It is a life of sacrifice to some degree; some of the modern comforts are just cost prohibitive and have to be left behind. I used a flip phone while living there since there was never enough internet or cell service to really justify anything fancier. To some, this is torture, not being connected to the rest of society so closely. But for others, myself included, to live in a place removed from the frantic churn of most of our lives was liberating. Moving away from Alaska the first time was painful. I stood on the stern of the Alaska ferry watching Kodiak and her snowcapped peaks sink into the distance with a pain in my heart that I had never felt before. Saying goodbye to the wildest of wild lands, and the life you lived while you were part of it, was hard, and being apart from it doesn't get easier with time either. Want to look into yourself? Spend some time in the backcountry of Alaska.

Chapter Three

Hawaii:
The Proving Grounds

In my eyes, Hawaiians are the best fishermen in the world. The ingenuity, pride, and cultural connection to the land and sea have always set the standard for me on a balanced life, well-lived. Hawaii is not an easy place to fish. Each island is surrounded by a ring of coral, which correspondingly has breaking surf, making open water access limited to certain channels. The warm, salty water eats any and all metal. The sea conditions can be demoralizing; don't believe the brochures, the weather here is often a beast. I am comfortable making the statement that I have seen more consistently better sea states in summertime Alaska than in summertime

Hawaii. Due to a nearly stationary high-pressure system to the northeast of the Hawaiian island chain, strong easterly "trade" winds are the norm. So, unless you live on the lee-ward side of the islands, be prepared to fish in some snotty seas.

The pristine, clear waters, although intoxicating to swim in, tell a story of the lack of plankton in the water. The lack of this basic building block in the food chain means that the total biomass just isn't as prolific as it is elsewhere. The rivers don't swell with salmon, or any fish for that matter, in Hawaii, as the fish stocks generally are just not as big. Each island is a desert oasis and every pelagic fish is a nomad.

To be consistently successful here sets an angler apart. The upshot is that the access to the big game species is mind-blowing. Upon clearing the harbor breakwaters, you can deploy your trolling spread for big pelagics. Although the fiftieth state in the US, there are many unique cultural practices that are codified into fishing that are unique to the islands. Like Alaska, Hawaii is isolated. Geographically speaking, it is the most isolated islands on Earth. This makes the fuel more expensive, the options for about everything less, and the adventure of it all just a little sweeter.

There are some amazing fisheries throughout the islands. Hawaiians created a method of fishing called slide-bait fishing to pursue ulua (giant trevally). Ulua routinely top one hundred pounds and are the premier fish for shore fishermen. To overcome the challenges of the lava coastline, which is prone to snags, slide bait fishermen purposely snag the bottom by casting out a sinker with wire arms like a grappling hook. With this main line secured, large baits like whole octopus, moray eels, or live reef fish are slid down the line.

To overcome the power of the mighty ulua, Hawaiian anglers have perfected the art of casting large conventional reels like Penn Senators, a feat that the rest of the country's anglers did not think was possible—to provide the line capacity and drag rating to keep up with these fish. Upon taking a strike from an ulua, the sinker breaks free and the angler battles the fish, often at night, from the rocks. Slide-bait fishing is usually an overnight event, including a camp setup with multiple anglers casting out as many as a dozen separate rods.

Assortments of vividly colored fish live along the reef, each one prettier than the next, and are pursued by both anglers and spear fishermen. On the sandy flats, schools of o'io (bonefish) search for their next meal. They are a popular food fish in Hawaii, often made into fish cakes by the local fishermen. At night, I enjoyed walking the reefs and shallow waters, armed with a three-pronged spear and flashlight, searching for octopus, known locally as "tako." But as fun as these activities can be, what the state is really known for is big game fishing.

Just beyond the reef line, monsters lurk. While most parts of the world require an extended boat ride to reach offshore grounds, in Hawaii they are literally just off the shore. Each island is the top of a large volcano, and it doesn't take long to reach the offshore abyss. While in New England, it would take me well over one hundred miles to reach the 500-fathom line (one fathom equals six feet), in Hawaii, I could do it inside of eight miles from any port I launched from. Once offshore, there were no safe havens. If your boat broke down, there was nothing but open water for thousands of miles. To run a boat over the horizon in Hawaii was not for the faint of heart. You had to know your bearings, know your boat, and find a way to get home.

The major species a fisherman trolls for in Hawaiian waters are: ahi (yellowfin and bigeye tuna over one hundred pounds), mahi-mahi (dolphinfish), ono (wahoo) and all Pacific species of billfish (blue, black, striped, spearfish, and sailfish). About the only species you won't find here are white marlin, as they are confined to the Atlantic Ocean. Like Alaska, fish here come with more than one name. There is the "mainland" name, the Hawaiian name, maybe a Japanese name, and sometimes a name based on the size of the fish. An example would be a skipjack tuna. Obviously, its common name is the skipjack tuna, its Hawaiian name is aku, but a big one over twenty pounds is called an "otado" or "otaru," which is actually a city in Japan. Likewise, an ahi would be a yellowfin tuna over one hundred pounds, while one under that size would be a shibi.

Cultural Differences

Hawaii is not just a state, it's an island nation. Local and native Hawaiians are proud of their heritage and seek to protect and perpetuate their culture against the never-ending barrage of commercialization of the islands. Apparently, everyone wants a piece of paradise. Being an outsider, a *haole*, it wasn't always easy to break in. But it takes a fisherman to recognize a fisherman, and I would also say Hawaiians are some of the most welcoming and generous people I have met. Aloha, the island greeting, is not just a salutation. It translates more closely to the "breath of life." Like gravity, it is easier to see the effects than the force. You give aloha and you get aloha. I have forged some of my deepest relationships on these islands, making close friends through the bond of being a waterman and fisherman.

At first glance you may not think there are seasons in Hawaii but after spending a year there, it becomes clear that there are. It takes more motivation to get into the water in winter than it does in summer. The seasons are felt both in terms of weather and fish. The ahi, ono, and big marlin arrive in the spring and stick around through the dry season (summer) to spawn. The mahi-mahi seem to surge in the fall and again in the spring. The rainy and cooler wintertime is slower, but striped marlin and spearfish appear in greater numbers. The seasonality is really only noticeable if you live here, but it provides a rhythm to follow.

With the exception of inshore reef fish and deepwater bottom fish, there are few licenses, size limits, or any real sense of regulations when it comes to offshore fishing in Hawaii. One's initial reaction is that regulations are needed to protect the species and to level the playing field. What I learned plying the waters here is that the playing field is level. On the world's most isolated rock, nomadic fish wander the currents of the Pacific. Fishermen depart from historic ports to troll the often-rough waters, using the same trolling techniques that have been employed for a century. Some of them, like deep dropping for tuna, in which anglers wrap their baited hook around a smooth rock, date back thousands of years.

Hawaii, as I see it, does not need many regulations because the ocean itself does a pretty good job of regulating the fishermen. I spent thousands of dollars on boats and sophisticated electronics only to find better success in following birds and looking for trash in the water when trying to locate where baitfish might be hiding. The inefficiency of trolling in mile-deep water, covering a seemingly barren sea, or straining your eyes for a bird pile regulates fishermen without much government intervention. That inefficiency, in my eyes, factors into the equation for fair chase.

Ancient Hawaiians had their own set of fishing restrictions, called *kapus*, which prohibited the taking of fish at certain times of the year, generally to protect spawning aggregations of inshore fish that were so crucial to their protein security. Being the most isolated islands on Earth with limited terrestrial animals to meet their protein needs, it was imperative to prevent overfishing of stocks and take only what was needed to subsist. Although they never crossed paths, early Hawaiians and native Alaskans have a lot in common. Skilled mariners, they both set out in small crafts onto big waters to intercept the seasonal migrations of fish that would come through their home waters with no guarantee of returning safely or finding the fish. A tradition from years past, Hawaiian boats still place the long leaves from the Ti plant in their rod holders as they set out to sea each morning to bring good luck and safe returns. I also appreciate the traditions of both locales of showing respect for the fish by using as much of it as possible; belly meat, eggs, cheeks, and even the collars (the thin horseshoe-shaped section of meat between the gills and pectoral fins) are all retained and little goes to waste as they share freely amongst their family and friends because the family, the *ohana*, the *du yinaanàx*, was and is still central to everything. I live my life by the same philosophy and these connections continue to draw me to both of these places.

Without intending to, Hawaiians have become the free-thinkers of fish retention. The result or maybe perk of being left alone in the Pacific for centuries with your main protein source having fins has caused Hawaiians to consider all fish as being created equal. Few fish are elevated to the status of being too holy to be eaten. Billfish, bonefish, and everything in between are fair game for food. This leveling of prestige is unique to Hawaii, and fish are judged by their table fare rather than gamefish status. Alaska's categories of fishing—commercial, subsistence, and recreational—are strictly separate; Hawaii rolls these three up into one. On most days, I would bet that a typical boat intends to touch on all three of those categories. With a simple state permit, anglers can sell pelagic (open water) fish for profit, even just a few to cover expenses, and bring home the rest to subsist off. It is a righteous concept, and I like it.

In an era of sustainability, eating local, knowing where your food comes from, and capturing fish on rod and reel are concepts that resonate. Fresh fish, caught by local, day-boat fishermen, is the antithesis to the industrialized fisheries found elsewhere. Much of the fish here is consumed raw, and having fresh fish is key to keeping it a positive experience for one's digestive tract. Pre-contact with Western cultures, Hawaiians' main source of protein was from the sea. Even today, the average American eats sixteen pounds of seafood a year. According to the University of Hawaii, residents of Hawaii consume twenty-eight and a half pounds a year.

Living in Hawaii opened my eyes to how good most pelagic fish tastes raw. One of the favorite local dishes is the poke bowl, which originated from fishermen in bygone days cutting the scraps of their catch for a quick snack and blossomed into a worldwide trend. Cubes of raw tuna, mixed with Hawaiian sea salt, green onions, soy sauce, sesame oil, and a host of other options are layered upon a bowl of rice. Today it is heavily influenced by many other Asian cuisines, but it remains one of the best meals I can imagine. It is so good that when I first experienced the taste, it was another strong motivator for me to become a commercial rod and reel fisherman.

That happened when life first took our family to Hawaii in 1988, when I was at the impressionable age of six. My dad received orders to assume command of the Coast Guard Cutter *Mallow*, a 180-foot seagoing buoy tender homeported in Honolulu. The ship would take him throughout the western and central Pacific Ocean and would serve as the vehicle to ingrain both offshore fishing and the Coast Guard into my very existence for the rest of my life. The ship's primary mission was to service the aids to navigation that mark the channels and shoals of the ocean. Knowing my interest in it all, my dad would often take me with him for shorter trips to experience it firsthand. Once I had proven that I could stay out of trouble and out of the way, he started taking me on longer trips as well. I would sleep on the deck of his cabin, help out around the ship, and, in exchange, got to fish off the stern.

Not surprisingly, for a kid that had never really been in rough seas, my first journey on the high seas did not go so well. Over the course of the weeklong trip, the likely ten-foot swells caused me to curl up on the deck for most of the trip, unable to eat much, let alone attempt to fish. But something clicked. Despite the physical misery of it all, I came home wanting to do it again.

When I was not fishing myself as a kid in Hawaii, I was watching or reading about how my childhood hero, Mike Sakamoto, was doing it. He was the host of Hawaii's all-time most popular fishing show, *Fishing Tales,* and author of numerous Hawaii-centric fishing books. Personifying the aloha spirit, he would frequent local tournaments and fishing events. My dad and Mike had become friends, bonding over fishing, and I remember the day he came over to our house for dinner. It was like meeting Paul Bunyan, Superman, and Santa Claus all in one, as he told stories and invited me to fish with him on future trips. I would write him letters in the following months to tell stories of the fish I caught. His weekly TV show was the highlight of my week, and I made sure I was there each Sunday afternoon to watch what he was fishing for. There may even be truth to the story that rather than miss a few moments of his show for a bathroom break, I went ahead and just pulled up a seat cushion and peed into the couch. Sorry, Mom, I do remember we sold that couch—buyer, beware!

I anxiously awaited an opportunity to fish with Mike, and fate did not disappoint. Several large weather buoys were positioned hundreds of miles offshore of Hawaii to provide mariners with on-scene weather conditions and help meteo-rologists with weather predictions. Although they were owned by the National Oceanographic and Atmospheric Administration (NOAA), the positioning and servicing of these aids fell to the Coast Guard. Additionally, placing a buoy seemingly in the middle of nowhere on the high seas created a Fish Aggregating Device (FAD) of the magnitude that few can understand. Pelagic fish have an affinity for floating objects, and a large buoy with thousands of feet of anchor chain was like a palm tree in the desert, a mini ecosystem. *Mallow* was tasked with servicing one of these buoys, and my dad invited Mike along. To my utter delight, he also invited me! I knew I would have a great day, but little did I know I was about to have, still to this day, *the* greatest fishing trip of my life.

The weather and seas were calm, nothing like my previous trip on *Mallow*. I distinctly remember how surprisingly nice the conditions were. After a few days of steaming offshore, we arrived at the large yellow buoy in the middle of nowhere. As the cutter surveyed the area, gauging the current, we made a few passes of the buoy, with lines out, of course. Mike and I stood in front of the center rod as the ship made the first pass of the buoy. As we approached, the reel started dumping line with a large mahi-mahi on the working end. Mike helped me turn the handle and we cranked the fish together until it was gaffed and brought over the side. After that, it was a blur of mahi-mahi and ono coming over the rail one after another.

We kept up this pace for an hour, and then there was the real Coast Guard work of replacing the buoy to be done. While the crew worked the buoy, Mike and I diamond-jigged off the port side of the ship. Wearing my Velcro shoes and life jacket, Mike taught me how to jig the rod, reeling up several feet if no hits were taken. Almost immediately, a sixty-pound bigeye tuna hit. With me weighing in at only sixty-five pounds soaking wet, I couldn't do much on the reel, but Mike coached me through it, and we gained on the fish. From there on, the entire crew was jigging and slaying bigeyes. There must have been two thousand pounds of tuna that hit the deck that day. Not having the strength to catch more than a few of these fish, my job was to club the tuna using a large pipe wrench as they hit the deck. I still recall being sprayed by blood as I worked on tuna crowd control. I kept the blood-splattered hat I wore that day as a badge of honor.

With the dust (blood) settled, I made two major life decisions right then and there: the first was that I had become an offshore fisherman, and the second was that I would join the Coast Guard once I grew up.

These convictions had been building within me for some time. At the ripe age of six, I began fishing local tournaments on O'ahu. With my dad gone on a deployment, my mom took me out one Saturday to fish off the rocks. Based on her advice, I went with a small piece of raw bacon as my bait of choice that day. I was not having much luck until I hooked this strange-looking fish that resembled a rock. As I was swinging it toward me to eventually remove the hook, a local fisherman came hustling over to tell me to not touch it. I had caught a stonefish, an extremely venomous fish that might have killed me if it had poked me. Deadly fish, big tuna—I was hooked on Hawaii, to say the least.

The time I spent growing up in Hawaii was impressionable. Fishing with Mike Sakamoto offshore left an indelible mark on me. I came back for summers and vacations but felt the deep need to move back. Maneuvering my professional life in my thirties, I was able to navigate my way back to the islands once again, thanks to a new assignment from the Coast Guard. Like a salmon wanting to return home to its river, I was going back to the place that had such a great impact on the course of my life—back to the motherland of offshore fishing. But first, I needed a boat—again.

Cashing in savings bonds and savings accounts, I thought I had a fair sum of money to put toward that goal. Boats, of course, are expensive, but I learned that boats are especially pricey in Hawaii, as the supply is limited but the demand is high. Finding a seaworthy hull, a well-maintained engine, and a corrosion-free trailer escaped me. In a place like the open seas off Hawaii, taking shortcuts on any of these three would not end well. After several months of fruitless searching, I found a twenty-foot center console, a "mainland boat," but it was in good shape, as was the engine and trailer. I swore I wouldn't buy another center console after running one in Gloucester. Hawaii-style boats are made from heavy fiberglass, with a distinct sharp and high bow to slice through the ever-present seas. The controls are elevated, usually on a flying bridge to provide for the driest ride and best visibility. Center consoles offer none of this. They provide little barrier from sea spray, wind, and waves, all of which are in play when trolling at eight knots in the notoriously rough waters around the islands. But it met my criteria, and I purchased it, renaming her the *Ohana o Kai*, translated to "Family of the Sea."

I then took to the task of preparing her for sea duty in Hawaii. I went through all aspects of the engine: starter, belts, oil, spark plugs, and anything else that might fail me. I started by replacing the batteries. Being a single-engine vessel, I had to be all in on this one engine, since there was no backup to bring me home. I loaded the boat with safety equipment and then set my sights on making this boat a fishing battle wagon. I intended to pursue big fish off this rather small boat and upon inspection, the gunwales (sides of the boat) were not ready to support a large rod and larger fish pulling on it. I removed the factory rod holders and installed vertical, swivel rod holders. This allowed the rod to pivot around 360 degrees as I fought a fish. Under the gunwale I bolted a one-inch mahogany board to act as a backing plate, so the rod holder would not rip out. The boat lacked outriggers as well. These are long poles that extend from offshore trolling boats and are a nonnegotiable item for serious offshore fishing. They spread trolled lures away from the boat, which allow more lines to be trolled simultaneously as well as lift the main line higher to keep the lure closer to the surface. Factory outriggers would run in the thousands of dollars to purchase and install. Having just dropped an uncomfortable amount of available cash on this boat, factory outriggers were out of the question. However, I had an idea. Hawaii's high country has dense groves of bamboo. Cured bamboo has been used in offshore fishing for years, and by repurposing it, it became the perfect do-it-yourself outrigger. She was finally ready to fish, she had a distinctive island flare, and it was time to get to work.

Offshore trolling is a unique method of fishing. Multiple lines are deployed beyond the boat at various distances, each lure and position deliberately chosen. The biggest surprise to newcomers is the speed at which the boat moves, usually six to ten knots. It is a fast clip, but with many pelagic fish able to sprint at speeds close to fifty knots, there is realistically no way of outrunning a fish. The second thing that will catch your eye is the size and beauty of the lures used. With a resin head roughly the size of a film canister and multiple rubber squid skirts tied to the back, these lures are an iconic part of Hawaiian fishing culture. Many are the length of an adult's forearm and it is sometimes hard to tell if a lure belongs in a shadow box or a tackle drawer. Armed with hooks that could tow a car and a leader with the thickness of weed wacker line, it is a sight to behold.

Hawaiian fishermen are in a league of their own and continue to set the standard by which the rest of the trolling world compares themselves. Local lure makers, spanning back several generations, dedicate their life's work to the pursuit of perfection in these lures. It is rare to see lures used in Hawaii that are not created in Hawaii. Walk into any tackle shop on the islands, and you will be amazed by the art forms that they call trolling lures, each head handmade by a local craftsman and equally appealing to both fishermen and fish. Local craftsmen like Ken Ching of KC lures, Eric Koyanagi of Koya lures, and hundreds of others create functional art from resin and sandpaper. It was Hawaiian anglers that invented the high-speed lure trolling and resin lure making that is now practiced worldwide. The art of lure crafting for offshore fishing runs deep in tradition in Hawaii and it is replete with heroes like Joe Yee, George Parker, and Henry Chee that border on legends.

By the time I moved to Hawaii I had become a competent lure maker, but wood is a forgiving medium, and carving a lure from wood is more about taking away then adding. Pouring resin is different. It's a medium I had never worked in. As a young kid, I actually broke a resin head lure apart just to see what was inside. To create a shape from a liquid, you must first create a mold, and then shape it with wet sandpaper. Resin, being clear, requires dyes and pigments to be added as well. In the center of any resin head lure is an insert, which serves as both the ballast and the primary visual attractant.

The creative combination of all these steps seemed an unsolvable riddle to me, and kept me as an outsider when it came to fashioning Hawaiian-style resin heads. Nevertheless, as I traveled the country, I always remained a Hawaiian-style fisherman. When I fished offshore around the mainland, I made it a point to troll Hawaiian-made resin heads. Unlike mass-produced plastic heads that most fishermen ran, the hand-turned Hawaiian heads stood out. They were shaped by a fellow fisherman, by hand, and they ran better. The mahi-mahi and tuna in New England never saw baits like this.

Working with resin remained a mystery to me until I came across Jim Rizzuto's famous book *Lure Making 101*. While I never met Jim in person, his articles and books fueled my passion and guided my development as a fisherman. I loved reading Mike Sakamoto's and Jim Rizzuto's articles on Hawaiian-style fishing and lure making, and as a seven-year-old, they served as my bedtime stories. I carefully reviewed over and over each how-to piece or tournament report and studied with rapture the lures hanging off the pectoral fin of the big marlin hanging at the weigh station in the article's photos.

Armed with Jim's book, I began creating molds from pill bottles, food containers, and anything else that caught my eye. I came to understand how the placement of weights, angles of the face, and length of the head all factored in to what the bait would do in the water. It took me until I was a grown man to crack the code, but with the aid of Jim's book, it was a transformational discipline to learn.

The timing of my growing hobby was good, as Renee and I were starting a family and time was not a luxury that either of us could afford. Pouring lures during a baby's naptime or after bed was a great way of finding balance. Resin work involves a lot of waiting: pour a layer of resin and wait for it to dry; pour another layer and wait again for it to dry. I could step out to the garage at naptime, do forty-five minutes of work, and then be ready to reengage on the home front. Now that I was back in Hawaii, I felt fortunate to be fishing these waters once again and using lure making techniques created on the islands. With no official off season in Hawaii, I had access to year-round testing for new lures to see how they ran and hopefully caught fish. My resin heads quickly began to increase in quality, and I am finally to the point of competing with store-bought baits for the fish's attention.

Working on a new shape for the weekend's trip gave me a sense of fulfillment that is beyond just catching a fish. It connected me with that long line of offshore fishermen who plied these waters before me. Generations of fishermen, from millennia past to as recent as Mike and Jim, created their own lures ahead of their next trip. I owed much of my offshore knowledge to Mike Sakamoto and Jim Rizzuto for passing on their craft. They touched many lives, made me a better fisherman, and, in Mike's case, set my life on a course that might not have ever happened if he had not taken the time to befriend a skinny kid with a relentless appetite for fishing knowledge. When I am working resin in the silence of the night after my kids have gone to bed, I think they would both look on approvingly that their craft continues, and I look forward to passing the same knowledge on to my kids, two of whom were born in Hawaii. Like its waters, Hawaii's fishing traditions run deep.

With my boat and my lures, I began in earnest to fish as hard as I could offshore Hawaii. But fishing the islands is not like anywhere else—it's harder, it's frustrating, and the end-of-the-day "mercy bites" are rare. I have never been humbled quite like I have been in Hawaii. I had to work hard to find the fish, especially with a smaller boat, and routine small-craft advisory on rough weather days. Each trip was a lesson in being able to read the Pacific and determine, in its vast emptiness, where fish would congregate. It was a skill that had to be earned. There are no shortcuts or apps, just miles under the keel.

It was the challenge that I had waited for. I became detail-obsessed to a fault. Each hook, crimp, piece of bait, and any other minutia was well thought out and reviewed. I would pore over nautical charts for hours, searching for a missed sea mount or ledge that would offer an unseen current line. I would fish for a full day, and if I saw a baitfish that didn't exactly match with my lures, I poured a new one in my garage to match the hatch. Through these efforts, I started catching fish. I was able to keep a steady supply of mahi-mahi and tuna in the freezer and prove to myself that I was doing something right.

But I needed that one big fish to be my diploma. That first season I went zero for six on billfish. The hook pulled on each fish. The one bit of pride I could take away is that I never lost one due to my gear failure. Marlin are notorious for being tough to hook, with their bony mouths and insane acrobatics. They are indeed a challenge. In talking with one well-respected skipper, he confided to me that he once lost twenty-seven marlin in a row before finally landing the twenty-eighth. Humbling!

I had some close calls where I thought for sure I was going to put a big one in the boat. I was still fishing by myself, but my interest in fishing offshore solo was inversely proportional to the addition of new children to our family. I was constantly pulled between the desire to run offshore and knowing that pushing the limits on a small rig would eventually catch up with me. Each morning, leaving the house at 3 or 4 A.M., I would look back at it from the front yard and ask God to bring me home to see it again in the afternoon. Each trip was an unknown, and by this point in my adventures, I knew nothing was guaranteed.

—◆—

Fishing Log: 21 August

Solo trip from Keehi to Waianae. Lost a marlin at the submarine cable off Barbers on a nine-inch plunger. Very rough coming home, sketchy. Took a kawakawa on the way in. Boat getting maintenance done.

I nearly had her. I took a day off work to troll off the west side of the island. Launching from the south end of the island in Honolulu, I ran clockwise around Barbers Point, a geographic feature named after a captain whose claim to fame was disregarding the weather and running his ship aground there one night. I liked fishing this area; it produced for me and I always felt lucky working these waters. From offshore of Barbers Point, I could see all the way up the Waianae coast as well all along the southern coast of the island. The steep drop-offs of the waters were really just the side of an underwater volcano that sloped down to thousands of feet over the lateral distance of just a few miles. If the winds came up, I could run back inshore toward the city before I got caught in them. But today, nothing came up into the spread. So, I kept going up the west coast of the island toward Nanakuli and Waianae. It was a gamble guessing the winds in the lee of the Waianae mountain range. I would enjoy calm seas but not know if the wind had come up until I made my way out of the mountain lee and back around Barbers Point. But every trip is a gamble, and I went for it. The seas were beautiful and there were some aku present, but none too cooperative up the coast. By midday, it was time to point the *Ohana o Kai* south and fish my way home.

As the mountains tapered down from the heavens to the sea, my old foe, the wind, showed itself. The mountains were to the left of me, and the wind poured over them. At this point, the winds and small whitecap waves were harmless to me because the sea had no fetch, which is the horizontal distance in which the wind impacts the water. I was still several miles from Barbers Point, and it was evident that once I came around the point, the sea would have all the fetch it needed to pommel me. Then I saw it: a pile of birds so thick it looked like black smoke.

A "bird pile" is the term offshore fishermen use to describe a flock of seabirds actively feeding on a school of baitfish. The baitfish are usually pushed up by predators below and trapped against the surface. With sight that I can best describe as X-ray vision, these terns, shearwaters, frigate birds, and boobies are able to see these schools of fish and dive into them. Most impressive are the boobies, which enter the water like a high-speed missile, diving deep to grab a fish before returning to the surface.

This pile was not huge but incredibly dense, like a black cloud. Along the 500-fathom line, it was exactly what I was looking for. I came to port and made my approach. Before even getting abeam of it, one of the outriggers came crashing down with a big strike. I was on something good and the Penn 130 was dumping line. Looking back in my wake, I saw a marlin jumping. Here we go! After a series of jumps the fish settled in and I began gaining line on it. Fighting the fish for twenty minutes, I was confident that if I made it this far, the hook must be buried. I moved between getting the harpoon and gaff ready and gaining line on the fish. I even had time to drop my dad a quick text to let him know I was tight on a fish.

As I was cranking the reel, keeping steady pressure, I can still recall the distinctive and discouraging pop as the rod went dead following a pulled hook. I couldn't believe it: it was gone.

The hook just came out. I worked the area a little longer, but the pile dissipated as the winds grew. It was time to take my lickings.

Naturally, I kept trolling as I rounded Barbers Point and saw the seemingly endless blue monsters awaiting my arrival. The seas had built substantially since this morning. I considered turning back to Waianae, but with my truck and trailer over an hour away, it would be a logistical pain. So I went for it. Drawing on my years of boat training, I throttle-jockeyed the boat over each wave, turning the wheel to slide down the backs of them. I started easing myself closer to shore and inside of Barbers Point so that in the event that I lost power or capsized, I would drift toward shore. It was an unsettling feeling to see my high water bilge alarm go off. I could not leave the helm to check, so I just hoped that my pump was keeping up with the water as I pushed the boat further. I told her, "If you get me back to the dock, I will get you some professional maintenance."

I forgot about the fact that I still had lines out until I heard one of my drags go off with a strike from a fish. "Sorry, but you're going to go for a ride." I finally reached the harbor entrance just after the third hour had gone by on a transit that should have taken an hour. Not until I entered the channel of the harbor could I reel in a very exhausted *kawakawa* (little tuna), which I happily gave away to a homeless man. The boat held up her end of the bargain, and I did take it to the shop for some preventative maintenance. The heartache of losing that fish caused me to examine every aspect of my gear, boat, and style of fighting. Defeat makes you a better student and makes victory taste a little sweeter when it finally arrives. Nothing worthwhile ever came easy to me, and big-game fishing in Hawaii was no exception. This wasn't a place where technological advances had a correlation to greater success. Knowledge was earned or passed on.

To that point, I became friends with Pat Murphy, a long-time fishing fixture in Waianae. While my boat, being just under twenty feet, couldn't push off as far to chase monsters, Pat's thirty-two-foot Blackfin Express could. Our first trip together was on my birthday. The trade winds were cranking that day and even in the lee of the Waianae mountains, the seas were churning. My hands hurt from holding onto the railing all day, but I liked that he was as crazy as I was about the pursuit of fish. He, too, subscribed to the ethos of being on the water well before sunrise to catch bait and be in position for the morning bite. Our trips together often resulted in everything from marlin to ahi. He, like any troller, was particular in his lure selections. Second to location, it was the biggest factor in determining success. When he selected one of my homemade lures to make it into his starting lineup, it was a big compliment. Pat taught me the intricacies of lure positions, skirt selections, and just how important it was to never stop trolling.

Hawaii has fifty-five FADs deployed across the island chain, ranging from three miles to thirty miles offshore. These buoys are specifically placed and maintained by the State of Hawaii to increase fishermen's success. Each one of these buoys supports a mini ecosystem, providing food, cover, and shade in the otherwise featureless sea. Mahi-mahi and ono love the

FAD buoys, and smaller tuna are often guests as well. Larger tuna and marlin, knowing where their food likes to hang out, are often not far away. The common practice is to troll past these buoys a few times and see if you get a knockdown on the way out to the offshore grounds. Usually after three passes it becomes clear whether anyone is home. For me, most of the time it seemed that the fish were not around, weren't interested, or someone had already caught them. I occasionally took a strike early in the morning, but otherwise it was often a swing and a miss. But as it turns out, when I slowed down, reeled in the big lures, and set out some small surface poppers, I found out just how many fish were there the whole time.

Fishing Log: 23 December

Jackpot. Fished Waianae on Pat's boat. Two aku, 2 shibi (1 70 lbs.), 1 150 lb. marlin. Slow trolled PILI poppers and Yozuris around the buoy. Marlin on an Akule. Most fish at sunrise.

The first time I tried this was two days before Christmas. I was fishing with Pat Murphy and our other friend Tommy that morning. We ran out to a local FAD and saw there were some birds and life around. Judging from the activity of the birds, it was obvious that there was excitement below the water, and we would be smart to stick around to see what would transpire. We slowed the engines down and slipped back several smaller lures as well. I dropped back a surface popper called a PILI popper forty yards behind the boat and began to methodically pop it. This lure is a uniquely Hawaiian surface lure. Originally designed by Peter Dunn-Rankin in 1982, the rights to the lure were bought by Mark Santiago in 1984, who modified the design and has been making them ever since. The lures are created from recycled surfboard foam and resin, and they are an iconic Hawaiian lure that reminds me of my childhood—Mike Sakamoto was the first person to introduce me to them.

It wasn't ten minutes of slow trolling the lure around the buoys with a heavy spinning rod in hand before I took the first strike. The aku and shibis were destroying the hot-pink plug. It was as if the lure was an insult to the fish, and they attacked it with an aggressive sense of purpose. At one point, what appeared to be an ahi crashed the lure so hard that the fish cartwheeled through the air. I watched the lure and the fish move in seemingly slow motion. At that same moment, a second large tuna attacked Tommy's lure and was boated after a long battle on light gear, with the hook bent nearly straight but still holding. We finished out the day by slow trolling a live akule (big eye scad) around the buoy, which a hundred-and-fifty-pound marlin found irresistible. It was a lesson of trying new techniques when you know there is life around. An ethos I like to use is "Don't leave fish to find fish." In this case, the fish were often there, they just needed a new lure and technique to be convinced to strike.

As I became better dialed in on Hawaiian-style fishing, an unrelated but awesome event occurred. My youngest brother, Patrick, moved to the island. Pat had earned his doctorate in physical therapy and came out to Hawaii to work. We hadn't lived near each other since I left home after high school, so it was a great experience to be so close. He was a top-rate fisherman and was ready to hone his offshore fishing skills alongside me. Finding a reliable fishing partner was no easy task, but with my brother now on island, we were a dream team. With absolute trust in each other, the scene was set for some big days.

Fishing Log: 09 October

One big mahi-mahi at MM buoy. Fished with Pat, got it on a PILI. Trolled 60 nautical miles. Two kawakawa at the point, found a glass ball too.

Our first good trip happened not long after his arrival. Fishing on the east side or "windward" side happened about once every two months for me. That was mostly because the days I had off usually did not coincide with the few days each month that the wind was not cranking. In a nineteen-foot boat, it didn't take too much to make it a rough ride. The weather on this day was about "meh." We took the occasional wave to the face, but it was not too sketchy. We started on the 40-fathom line for ono. Finding none, we slid out to the 500-fathom line in search of something bigger; still nothing. So, we pointed her east toward the 1,000-fathom and much to our chagrin, still found nothing. It was the point at which we either made it our excuse or doubled down. To our southeast and upwind at another eight miles was a FAD buoy. Patrick indicated that "we were practically there," so, with an eye toward the slightly building and untrustworthy waves, I pointed the *Ohana o Kai* into the seas.

After another hour and with Oahu looking very small on the horizon, we spotted this lone buoy bobbing in the ocean, with nobody around. I fully expected this thing to be holding a ton of fish. I made our first pass on the buoy and . . . nothing. Not a good sign. It was a weekday and having seen no other boats all day, I was pretty confident that the buoy had not been picked. We took four more passes and the anticipation turned to disappointment, with a sprinkling of F-bombs. But I hadn't yet tried all my tricks. We slowed to three knots and broke out spinning rods and PILI poppers.

Again, we ran a star pattern past the buoy and was dismayed that out here in eight-thousand-foot-deep, without a boat in sight, we couldn't get a bite. On the last down swell pass on the buoy, Pat's popper got hit. Out of the water came a big cow mahi-mahi. I suppose we just pissed her off with the poppers going overhead to the point where she had to strike to remove this small pink intruder from her domain. Pat was in for a fight. I kept the bow down swell and tried to get the fish away from the buoy before it wised up and used it to cut us off. After some remarkable jumps the fish settled in, but did not want to close the gap. With the boat moving forward at clutch ahead, we couldn't apply enough heat with a spinning rod to move her in, so I had to de-clutch once in a while and wallow in the seas to allow Pat to close the gap. The mahi begrudgingly gave in, and we finally had her off the port quarter, holding steady, eight feet away. I went with my long, homemade bamboo gaff and stuck her behind the head. Fully stretched out, I realized my leverage wasn't that great and the fish pulled me back as much as I pulled her forward. I dragged her up the left side of the engine and wrestled the fish into the boat. Fuel and steering hoses are not the best of friends with a sharp gaff. Plus, the fish was shaking violently with a free double hook looking for purchase. Seeing this, I quickly got her into the boat's cockpit, luckily without puncturing the fuel line. In the boat, the fish went berserk. Mahi-mahi, while known for their beauty and taste, are also infamous for going nuts once boated. This one was no different. She was violently shaking, with multiple hooks hanging from her jaw. I jumped up on the seat and with the bat in my hand, began swinging, striking the fish to compel it to calm down. Commitment to the technique paid off on a buoy that I would have bailed on a year ago. Coming home we even found a large glass fishing float, a relic from Japan where a generation ago glass balls were used to float nets. It had likely been adrift for decades and was a rare find.

Pat picked up offshore fishing quickly. With minimal words, we were able to anticipate each other's actions and be successful. We often launched out of Waianae. We would leave my place at 4:30 A.M., get the boat from the storage lot, and trailer it over the mountain range to Waianae, approximately an hour's drive. On the leeward side of the island and at the base of the Waianae mountain range, it was the only place on the island where a consistent lee from the wind was possible. For a small boat fisherman, this is key and well worth trailering for an hour to take advantage of it.

Fishing off the windward side where we lived, I felt like I caught more fish. They were not always big ones, but I could usually find something. This was because of the currents that swept down the eastern side of the islands, often bringing with them various flotsam. Waianae was a boom or bust spot for us. If we hooked up, it was often a fish of consequence, but there were rarely any mercy bites, no participation trophies or consolation prizes. For us, to fish Waianae meant to go all in.

———

Fishing Log: 23 April

Lost one marlin off Waianae. Launched at 0615, had the hit at 0715 in 1400 feet of water, inside of "R" buoy on a purple seven-inch plunger. Nothing else. Trolled up to Kaiana Point. Weather kind of sucked.

Our first trip there didn't go so great. The harbor is prone to a sizable ocean surge. Backing the boat up the first time, a local man said something to me, which I didn't understand at the time, but in hindsight, he was telling me that the ramp I chose was the shallowest, with decent ocean surge. What he tried to tell me was that it was going to be sketchy. Sure enough, I quickly realized that there were actual waves breaking against the back of my 4Runner! I backed the boat down and quickly pushed it off the trailer, and Pat took control of her with the mooring lines. I yanked the trailer out before I got into serious trouble. I had limited knowledge of the harbor area or beyond, but we pushed out at sunrise into the sizable swells and readied our gear. We were already in 500 fathoms (3,000 feet) at a mile out from shore, so we deployed our spread of lures.

With four lures splashing and popping correctly, it was not more than ten minutes before we spun around at the sound of an Avet 50 class reel dumping line. Behind us, a small marlin had taken a purple seven-inch plunger I had created and was tail-walking across the wake. It was gone before we could even take action. The hook hadn't found the right spot, likely, it was just hooked around the fish's bill. But it was action, and we thought it was the start of something epic. However, as the hours rolled by, it became apparent that we were to have just that one opportunity that day. Trolling for seventy-five additional miles yielded nothing, and we had a long afternoon of retracing our path across the island to reset.

Regardless, we were undeterred and building momentum. Like anywhere else, the more we fished the leeward side, the more we began to unwrap its secrets. There were big fish just beyond the breakwater. Trolling off Hawaii often feels like trying to intercept a missile with another missile. You are moving at eight knots, hoping to cross paths with another large animal doing the same. My family and close friends knew how much I put in, month after month, to this discipline. But if you want something bad enough, hard work and dedication are the entering arguments. With my hooks, leaders, and boat ready for battle, the table was set for the biggest fish I have ever crossed.

Fishing Log: 30 April

The big one. 611 lb. marlin off Barbers Point, in vicinity of 500–fathom line. Nine-inch chrome bullet on the long corner. Dad and Pat were onboard. One hour before low, loose white birds around. Five-hour fight. F/V Sea Hawk helped tow it in. Sold for $1.10/ pound.

The Marlin

It was a trip that almost didn't happen. My parents came out to help me watch the kids while Renee was away on Maui for a girls' weekend. I decided to take Monday off as well, probably burning some capital at work, to spend one more day with the folks. Pat had off on Mondays. In talking to a charter fishing friend, Jeff, he said the bite off Barbers Point was good, and on that day, the winds were unusually out of the west, opposite of the normal trade winds. Jeff told me he had lost an estimated seven-hundred-pound marlin the day before, after two hours of fighting. I replied, "You can keep those big marlin, I am just looking for some ono." My dad, Pat, and I trailed across the island along the empty H-3 highway well before dawn, noting the full moon, Mars, and a sky full of stars. Arriving with just the slightest hint of day, we launched out of Keehi Lagoon near Honolulu, then transited another fifteen miles to fish the deep ledges off Barbers Point. The last time I fished the area didn't go so well. I lost a marlin on a solo trip and got clobbered coming home by the seas. This time would be different.

I was hoping that with our dad along, luck would shine upon us and end our dry spell. We trolled west along the 40-fathom line for ono and after two hours had nothing to show. I pointed *Ohana o Kai* out a little farther offshore. I was surprised we had not crossed paths with at least one ono, but that's fishing.

The weather was great, the sun was out, and I was in good company. I said a small prayer, asking God to bless us with a fish, knowing full well that the big man upstairs likely had more pressing matters to contend with. But still, I wanted to have Dad hook up with something. He later told me he too asked for some divine intervention. I swapped out the ono lures for ones better suited for marlin and tuna. I called an audible by adjusting my usual spread, deploying a big, heavy, nine-inch jetted-chrome head with three skirts. It was a lure Pat Murphy had taught me to keep in the mix.

I don't think God does anything small. As we crossed the 500-fathom line, the long corner rod, with that nine-inch jetted-chrome bullet on it, exploded! The release clip that held the line sounded like a rifle going off as it snapped. The Penn International 130 started dumping. I have two 130s— the biggest reels on the market and, most of the time, an over-kill. I had thought about selling one recently but at least on this day I was glad I hadn't. Earlier in the morning, Pat and I were talking about the handle of the 130s and the fact that they were titanium. We made a comment about needing that level of strength, a foreboding observation. The fish ran for about thirty seconds, enough to tell me it was a fish of consequence, and then the line briefly slowed and stopped. I thought,

"Hmm, maybe not so big." I was thinking spearfish or striped marlin. Then, off the starboard beam of the boat, a big marlin came out of the water, paralleling our course and seemingly getting ahead of us. It almost didn't look real. We just stared at it as it walked on its tail, shaking its head wildly, trying to rid itself of this steel in its jaw. Pat actually asked if that was our fish. My dad quickly pushed down on the throttles to stay ahead of it.

We started clearing lines and stowing the deck. The fish just didn't stop. With it now once again behind us, it took more line that I had ever seen a fish take. Two weeks before, I felt this need to re-spool my reels as it had been about a year since I last did it. I really didn't want to, but knew that I had to. From re-spooling, I knew I had 326 yards of 150-pound mono top shot. That went flying out. Beneath that was approximately 500 yards of 200-pound braided line, of which at least another 300, maybe more, yards of line went out. Braided line, with its thinner diameter and anti-rot properties, is ideal for backing. I had never been taken into my backing before on this reel. I was now staring at the bottom third of the spool. Pat was getting antsy as we continued to lose a lot of line, and it was time to start recovering some. Dad drove, maneuvering the boat to keep the fish off the starboard quarter again. We kept the speed up, at least five knots for a while, turning in a clockwise pattern as both we and the fish maneuvered for best position.

This fight was about shoulder strength, seamanship, and horsepower. We were jacked up and rolled back a few thousand years in our language and attitudes. I had Pat on the reel initially. Putting those CrossFit muscles on the winch was no accident. As fatigue set in, I jumped in to keep the heat on. We were recovering line and this brute of a fish was steadily coming in. Dad jumped on next to keep the pressure up. My boat, rod, and leaders had never been tested like this before. The reel clamp, which provides an additional contact point on the bottom of the rod, fell off. I couldn't believe it. The reel was loose, and I wildly turned the rod clamp. It spun so much I assumed it was broken. It wasn't, but this rod had never been under so much pressure, even with me using a wrench to tighten it earlier.

After forty-five minutes, I started to prep the harpoon, thinking that we would soon have the fish boat-side. Dad then said something that I hoped wasn't true: "We have a few hours before this fish is ready." "No," I said, "It's coming in." But he was right. At about one hundred yards to go, I think she (big marlin are always females) had a quick look at the boat and took off again on another hard run, diving deep. Out went the 326 yards of monofilament and then at least an extra 300 to 400 yards of backing. Because of the angle that she dove, we couldn't use the boat to gain an advantage. I couldn't believe it. I thought that because of the jumping, she had filled her swim bladder and couldn't go deep. I was wrong. She was down to at least 1,500 feet in familiar Pacific water, where she caught her breath. Marlin were supposed to stay on the surface, burning precious energy with acrobatics, not fight like a tuna down deep. It became a standoff. The fish was down in the cool, dark, well-oxygenated water catching her breath. She was resting, settling in, and waiting us out. She slowly swam along, occasionally shaking her head, but swimming across the current toward

Diamond Head, maybe on a course that she thought would take her to safety.

Hour two passed. By this point, the fun had started to wear off and we all settled in, fighting in shifts but gaining little. I felt the need to quote Hemingway from *The Old Man and the Sea* as I put my entire body into the reel: "Fish, I love you and respect you very much. But I will kill you dead before this day ends." We would slowly gain a few feet of line but then lose it, as she was at equilibrium at that extreme depth. Close to hour three we felt confident that the fish was either dead or at least dying. We didn't know it at the time, but the hook was through her lower jaw from the outside in with the twenty-eight pounds of pressure keeping her mouth forcibly shut, likely suffocating her. This gamble by her to go deep was a suicide pact, either shake the hook or die trying. She did the long, slow dive. In hindsight, this was her death spiral.

The line was vertical, the pressure was constant, and our drift was with the current. Now it was a matter of winching it up from the depths. Initially, we were fighting the fish with one person, but the strength it took to pull the main line with your gloved left hand and then reel with your right was exhausting. Dad had an idea that we pull as a team: one guy pulling the line, one guy cranking, and the third guy working as a counterweight on the other side of the boat while at the helm. We rotated this shift for the next hour. Despite wearing gloves, the two-hundred-pound braid cut through to our hands. We applied strips of duct tape over forming blisters and cuts, pushing through the pain.

Dad has this old story about a big marlin he lost back in the 1980s, and it seemed a fitting time to tell it to Pat as we continued grinding in the hot sun. While captain of the *Mallow*, he was in Micronesia on a port call. He and two other crew members had gone out on a local skiff for some trolling. During the trip, they hooked a monster marlin. The old-school Penn Senator screamed as they devised a way of fighting the fish from an open boat without a rod holder, eventually ending up sitting on the deck against a bench. After hours, the fish, which was the length of their boat, was finally near: a huge black marlin. With the leader just out of reach, the line parted. It was a good fight, and he said the fish deserved to win the battle. A cold, heavy rain started falling as they made their way back to the island.

Thirty years later, he was doing the same thing all over again. Stories shifted to Mike Sakamoto, who had by now crossed the bar to troll the heavens. We asked him out loud to look down on us and lend a hand. Statistically, we should have lost this fish. It should have thrown the hook during her jumps, or shredded the leader with her bill, or snapped the line with her tail, or simply had the hook rip out as we slowly winched her up. We had unknowingly killed this beauty in the battle and wanted to stay with our mantra that if you take a fish—you keep it!

I kept saying that we should be into the mono soon. With the braided backing stretched tight, the line provided little hint of when it would ever end. The mono would signify we were 326 yards away, and its thicker diameter would provide needed relief to our hands. But it seemed to never end. The man on the reel just kept staring down into the blue water with a blue line trailing into the abyss. It was so tight that at one point Dad strummed the line, which I didn't appreciate, and it sounded like a guitar. Then we saw it, like a lighthouse in a storm—the mono to braid connection. A beautiful sight, now "only" 326 yards to go. We pushed on, knowing that we were getting closer, all the while slowly drifting out to sea. We were all getting tired and sluggish. The sun was high, and we wallowed in the large swell off the port beam. I was glad I always pack for a full day, bringing far more water and food than normally anticipated. We gulped down the water. I realized that the sun had already passed its highest point and was now coming down the other side of the sky. We hooked the fish at 9 A.M. I looked at my watch and looked at Dad. We both knew that at 2 P.M. we were going to have to hustle to beat sunset.

The afternoon wind started to rise as the heated land caused the sea breeze to pick up, which in turn caused a chop on the water in addition to the already big swell. As the huge fish got closer to the surface, the weight of it became greater, and the reduced amount of line out resulted in less shock absorption. The spool was filling up nicely; we had to be getting close. The swells now played a leading role in the fight. We had to try to hold what we had as the boat gently rose up, and then reel like hell coming off it. I had the drag slightly past strike and cupped the reel with all my strength to hold onto what we got. We gauged each swell, sometimes veering out just a little line to prevent it from parting. The gunwale of my boat, which had been flexing and producing sounds like no gunwale should, started overtly creaking and it sounded like it was about to break. We tried to keep at least one foot on it at all times. She was close now; I could feel it.

Then my heart sank. We saw something big off the stern, cruising just below the surface and looking like a green/white glow. "Oh, please don't let this be a shark," I prayed. It was large and interested in us. Once again, my thoughts went to Santiago from *The Old Man and the Sea*. With the fish close and a potential predator nearby, Pat and I went into beast mode. The rod, line, gunwale, and anglers were all at max and close to breaking. I was waiting to feel the soul-crushing pop as something gave; this was not sustainable. We saw the now multiple unknown predators again, this time closer. It was a race. Then we saw her, coming nose up—a monster marlin, bronze in color, and dead. I grabbed the leader as Pat stuck her with the harpoon. Then someone put a gaff in her. As she floated belly up, I grabbed the bill and held on as Dad got a line to put over the bill and another around her enormous tail. I held onto the fish, nearly eye to eye, and was fully expecting to see a pair of shark jaws until a rope came over my shoulder and I slipped it over her bill and cleated it.

I have never seen three guys show less emotion over a monster fish. We were wiped out. The fish stretched most of the length of my nineteen-foot, ten-inch boat. We just stood and stared at it. I tapped Dad's shoulder and extended my hand; we both laughed and shared a firm shake and a hug. Pat, meanwhile, started throwing up on the portside. I had used him up; he crossed the finish line and collapsed. Our initial, conservative weight guess was two hundred and fifty to three hundred pounds. She floated belly up, so it was hard to guess with any accuracy. We then started throwing ideas around on how to bring her aboard or in tow. We tried to lift her and she literally only rose a mere four inches. We talked about gutting her in the water to lighten her, but that would have made a nice chum slick for the still present sharks.

Side tow it was, and we lashed her alongside and started making our way back to the dock. We were doing maybe three knots and it was now past 3 P.M. with fifteen miles to go. It was going to be a late night. Then we saw salvation in the form of a white charter boat about a mile away. I called her on the radio. Sure enough, the F/V *Sea Hawk* answered. I explained our situation, and she gladly came about to help.

The captain, Daryl, asked how big she was. I radioed back two-fifty, maybe three hundred. He then asked how long we were fighting it. I said since 9 A.M. I heard him laugh, and he said, "Yeah that's bigger than 300." As the *Sea Hawk* approached, we attached a line to the marlin's bill and a poly-ball fender to the tail and threw the line over in the now-rising sea. My dad adroitly maneuvered alongside our salvation partner. We stood in amazement as three crew members of the *Sea Hawk* struggled to pull our catch in through their tuna door. It wasn't until that moment that we finally got a good look at her. This was a big fish! Daryl called over to tell us that the length and girth measurement worked out to 114-inches fork length and 64-inch girth, giving us an estimate of 585 pounds!

Once the fish was over, we picked up speed toward our launch ramp at Keehi. The plan was to recover our boat, then drive to Kewalo Basin a few miles away to collect the fish.

We left the marlin in the capable hands of the *Sea Hawk* and pointed the *Ohana o Kai* toward the dock. And, of course, I threw out a line for an ono on the way back—just in case.

By the time we got in, the winds had picked up and we were thankful the unusual west winds were behind us. I was coming into the dock a bit fast and went to check my speed by backing down and the engine cut out. We nearly hit the rocks but luckily reached out an outrigger to a guy on the dock, who happened to be standing there, to slow us down. Divine intervention again.

We cleaned up the boat as fast as we could and raced over to Kewalo Basin but the *Sea Hawk* and the marlin had beat us in. Pat noted how it felt like we were late to our own wedding. My mom, Renee, and the kids had come down as well and were there waiting for us. Pat was directing my mom via cell phone as to where to locate the *Sea Hawk* when she interrupted him, blurting out, "Oh my God, is that your fish?" She was staring down the dock at a brute of a fish, already strung high. Later that night, she described the sight of this enormous creature as nothing less than "profound."

By the time Pat, my dad, and I arrived, a crowd had gathered, including my two good friends Jimmy Garland and Adam Disque, who came straight from work to see it. I must confess, we felt a bit like celebrities pulling up. I couldn't believe how big it was: 611 pounds on the scale! It was the fish of a lifetime. I just stood there in awe of this sixteen-foot-plus fish. After a ton of photos, we made the decision to sell it. Pat and I gutted and gilled it in preparation to take it to the fish auction. I had kept an active commercial fisheries permit in my back pocket, just for an event like this. Daryl had convinced us that we should put this fish in a truck, not back into the boat, to transport it over to the Pier 38 auction block. Our only option was Adam's little Sport Trac pickup; beggars can't be choosers. We backed it up and lowered the fish in. The tail extended up above the cab and the head was well past the tailgate. It was a sight to see cruising down Ala Moana Boulevard, Oahu's main street, at rush hour!

We headed over to the fish auction block as a group. Despite the cantankerous security guard, who wasn't at all pleased to see us pulling up with an oversized sized fish on an undersized truck, we got the fish onto a pallet jack and into two thousand pounds of ice. I wanted to keep a piece of this fish, but selling it requires the angler to leave all the meat intact. I did, against counsel, take the bill and the tail. These were mine. We buried it in ice and left it there. Leaving the marlin behind was strange—I felt like I needed more time with this fish. I had fought it for five hours and had only briefly seen it before transferring it to the *Sea Hawk*.

My parents, Renee, Pat, the kids, and I had a nice dinner out as a family and took a moment to reflect on the momentous events of the day. Afterward, the three of us towed the boat back across the island, once again in the dark, remarking how the full moon was on the rise and Mars was visible.

For the fish to sell, it has to make forty degrees core temperature in twenty-four hours. The fish arrived with a core temperature of sixty-eight degrees: incredibly cold given the battle in the warm Hawaiian waters. She had spent so long down deep in the cold waters I am convinced it took off at least twenty degrees. We missed the final temperature reading the next day by two degrees. This caused a required listeria test to be administered and another day of waiting. I was restless and anxious. What if it didn't sell? How would I get it home? How would I process it all? There is no greater sin for a fisherman than to waste fish, especially such a regal fish as this. For two nights I tossed and turned. If the fish didn't sell, what would I do? I decided that if I had to pick up the fish and bring it home, I would call the radio station and advertise free Marlin to anyone who wanted some, handing it away as fast I could from my front yard.

Pat and I went down to the auction block on Thursday morning, hoping to perhaps see it sold. We were two new faces in the crowd and too tall to not stick out. Our presence was not exactly appreciated. We saw that great fish in a back freezer room. It had been cut in half and looked like two logs from a giant tree. We snuck a quick photo with her that almost got us kicked out. If it didn't sell, they would call me. I kept my phone close all day. They never called.

I slept only a little better that night and woke up promptly at 5 A.M. to call the auction block when they opened. "Boat name?" asked the voice. "*Ohana o Kai,*" I replied. Yes, your marlin sold yesterday for $1.10/pound. I ran in and woke Renee: "She sold!" It was more than a fair price. She would be consumed happily and locally and all was right and I wouldn't have to try to process it all by myself. It struck me at that moment that I had finally become a commercial fisherman.

I had been waiting for this fish all my life. I had maneuvered my whole life to get to Hawaii, bought a boat, and weaponized her from a sandbar queen to an offshore fisherman's dream. Hawaii knocked me down initially. She made me work for every bite. I spent hours and hours in my garage, re-tying every leader, obsessing over each hook point, and taking my reels down to the bearings. I laid in bed at night reviewing how I would fight this fish, and how I would land it. When she hit, I knew every connection between my hand and the fish was solid. I knew how to maneuver the boat, as I had practiced it numerous times. To have had my dad and brother onboard for this bite is something I can't quite put into words. It worked out; everything worked out. Big fish are normally lost. This time, by an unknown combination of skill, luck, and help from above, we got her. This fish was a big deal for me, it was the reward for all those hours and days I put in. When I see the bill of that fish that I have displayed in a shadow box now, it is physical proof that if you want something, and dedicate yourself, you can earn it.

Fishing Log: 01 July

Landed a 50 lb. spearfish. And lost a marlin. Launched out of Waianae. On with Pat. Pushed out to the Pinnacles. No life, turned toward Barbers Point. Took a marlin strike on a seven-inch bullet. Lost it. Also hit a nine-inch plunger on the short corner. Lost again. Took a spearfish outside of the buoy on the 700-fathom line on a nine-inch tube plunger in mahi-mahi colors off a bird pile on the short corner. Also hit the bird. Just past a full moon, low tide.

After landing that marlin, I fished with a diploma in hand and more confidence as well. We were battle-tested and relaxed. As the famous saying goes, "Time and tide wait for no man," and we both knew time was not on our side. Pat had steered his life toward the Air Force and was awaiting his rendezvous with officer basic training. I likewise knew my time on the islands was winding down, at least in the short term, so we fished with a sense of meaningful haste. The usual brotherly arguments were extinguished, and we just focused on making memories, knowing that it would be a while before we got to fish together again like this. With the winds cranking on the Kaneohe side, we decided to seek calmer seas and trailer to Waianae the day after my thirty-fifth birthday. Pat trailered the boat down one of the deeper ramps to launch and I efficiently slid it off and waited for his arrival from parking. We were regulars now, talking with fellow fishermen in the dark as we all prepared our machines for the day. We were out of the harbor in no time and looking for action.

Heading down the coast, we raised a large marlin in the spread. She was lit up and looking to attack. First, she hit the "shotgun" lure, the bait positioned farthest back. The reel dumped line, but the fish quickly came off. The fish then jumped out of the water like a porpoise and charged the boat, first at fifty yards, but each leap brought her closer, to the point where I expected the next one to result in the fish jumping right into the boat. I had never seen this behavior before. The fish was so close by the last leap that I could clearly look down its mouth and see its gills. Yards from the boat, the fish broke left and smashed the short rigger lure. As the line began to dump out, the fish released the lure once again. Pat and I both began to reel hard and then kick the reel into free spool, imitating a bait trying to escape and then falling behind. It worked. The fish grabbed my lure on the free spool and I let it run for a few seconds to ensure she had it. I slammed the reel into gear, but was surprised when the fish quickly got rid of it again. This demon fish was just playing with us and bill wrapping these hooks for the sport of it. After a period of time, she just disappeared back into the blue abyss and was gone. It was musical chairs with a marlin.

As the sun grew higher, we knew our chances for redemption were getting thin. We kept hammering the area, but it was in vain, and we couldn't raise another fish. By the afternoon, it was time to point the *Ohana o Kai* toward the dock. Each passing mile lowered our chance at a fourth-quarter mercy bite, which didn't exist anyway, especially on the Waianae side. Four miles from the dock, the sky grew overcast and the wind came up. Whitecaps built on the water as the weather started to change. Then we saw it, a beacon of hope for us: a bird pile. The black shearwaters, known locally as "matoris," were incredibly excited about something. This area often held small aku, and seeing these birds and the speed at which they were working indicated to me that it very well might be aku below. The freshening wind and sea spray seemed to add to the drama of it all as we maneuvered for an approach. Pat had the wheel and worked to keep the boat on the outside of the pile but would turn once past the pile to pull the lures through it. We kept our eyes on the rod with the small aku lure on it, so we were caught off guard when the 130 on the portside with the homemade nine-inch inverted plunger began to dump line.

I jumped on the reel to begin the fight. Typically, our system was that I took over the driving duties when we had a fish on, while Pat was the reel man. This time, Pat said, "No, you reel this one in." It was a fun change of duties for me. The outrigger release clip was set too tight, so as the fish ran, the outrigger was flexed down to the water's edge. I quickly hauled down the outrigger's line and tripped the release with a swipe of my hand. I started to gain line on the reel. By this point, the fish had stopped running, but the initial run told me it was still something of consequence. As I tell anyone new to offshore fishing, "If the line isn't going out, it should be coming in," so I took my own advice and began cranking. The fish was about one hundred and fifty yards out and tracking in nicely.

Pat kept the boat moving ahead slowly to ensure tension in the line, and I began to see the swivel coming into view. "Deep color!" I yelled, when I saw an electric blue and silver fish slowly coming up from below. I grabbed my trusty gaff made from bamboo in my left hand and took leader wraps with my right. It was either an ono or spearfish based on its size and color. As it came up directly behind the engine, I reached as far back as I could with my left hand and buried the gaff into the fish's shoulder. Its weight, combined with the forward speed of the boat, nearly took me off balance as I leaned back into the boat. Over the transom, the fish hit the deck and the hook popped out of its mouth. It was a shortbill spearfish, or *hebi*, as they are called locally.

It was the most elusive fish that I caught in Hawaiian waters. They are common nowhere, but seem to show themselves more in Hawaii and off the coast of Portugal than anywhere else. This was a larger one, close to fifty pounds. Its miniature bill and electric blue back was beautiful. Hebi are among some of the best tasting fish. This one would be enjoyed for several months. Waianae, after all our struggles, gave us a mercy bite and a good memory to hold onto for two brothers who had grown a deep appreciation for its waters.

At six years old, Hawaii had set my life on a course, but that was perhaps the most impactful year of my life, ingraining the culture of Hawaiian-style fishing into me. It is a rich and proud place and home to some of the world's premier watermen, mariners, and diehard fishermen who take big risks to catch big fish.

Chapter Four

Eating off the Grid without Going off the Deep End

(A Manifesto for the Modern Outdoorsman)

S o where does this all end for the guy who gets up hours before sunrise to pursue fish on his off time? For me, it is balancing the benefits of the modern world while enjoying, to the maximum extent, the fish I catch. Another term for it would be "subsistence harvesting." Although thankfully, the advances of the twenty-first century in food production and distribution have given us freedom from the do or die element of subsistence harvesting, it also robbed us of a primal tie to the land and its dietary resources. There is no real need to pack a freezer full of fish for the winter ahead, or even plant a garden in your yard. But then again, something about it sure feels right. Before I go down this road, I have to say, I am a huge proponent of catch and release. It is crucial to many fish stock's survival, and I don't take the harvesting of fish lightly. But, if I am short on fish, and the right kind are biting, I am going to make hay and get that fish in the freezer. With the demands of a growing family, and what once seemed like endless time now being a bit more precious, I look to make trips productive and harvest a few fish if feasible.

I always appreciated being my own provider and had even studied the concept a bit through college, but it was not until I moved to Alaska and Hawaii that I grew mindful of the philosophy behind the practice. Subsistence harvesting is the process of fishing or hunting as the primary means of providing the protein in your diet. There is recreation and enjoyment in the process, which is, of course, an added bonus. In Alaska, it was not an esoteric or New Age fad but rather a publicly accepted activity, complete with a full set of state laws to both support and protect it. This down-to-earth, "Yeah, that's the way we do it here" mentality was lockstep with what I had been searching for in terms of the fish and animals I caught or hunted and my relationship to the food I ate. Although not codified into conservation laws as much in Hawaii, the same was true. To live off the sea by your own hard work was valued and pursued. Providing for your family and neighbors was a virtue and mark of a true fisherman, and these true fishermen kept their freezers stocked with fresh fish.

Happiness is Filling the Freezer

It was in my teenage years and early twenties in New England that I began to appreciate providing wild-caught food for myself. It was usually in the form of seafood, but whether it was crabs, shrimp, fish, or lobster, it was always more fulfilling to have captured it myself. I developed an unwritten set of guidelines, maybe evolving into a personal code, if you will, that has grown as the years have gone by: Try not to eat fish you didn't catch. If you do eat store-bought, avoid farm-raised seafood, and never take a fish that you don't intend to eat. If I brought in an abundance, more than I needed, I would share with my friends and family. It was fun! It continued to cultivate my connection to the outdoors, and most importantly, gave me a deep sense of fulfillment.

Moving to Alaska afforded me an immersive dive into providing for myself. All food there had to be flown or trucked in and then barged to the island, making the cost of everything higher. In addition, supplies were not guaranteed. In winter, big storms sometimes kept these supply boats from making the transit, and fresh food in particular would be scarce until the seas calmed down. Most every fisherman and hunter I knew sought to ensure that they harvested enough fish and game to last until the next season. As mentioned earlier, Alaska regulates three basic categories of harvesters: commercial, recreational, and subsistence. The last was allowed in "remote" sections of the state, in areas away from any appreciable human populations. That simple license provided generous limits of fish. Methods such as gill netting and long lining, typically closed to recreational fisherman, were allowed. My new life in Alaska happily morphed into trying to harvest enough fish and game to make it to the next season, but not more.

Imperceptibly at first, I began to feel more connected to the natural pattern of life. Subsistence harvesting lashed me to the tides, the moon, and most importantly, the migration of animals. Knowing the sockeye salmon run was only six weeks long ignited the race to sustainably capture the correct amount of fish to last through the winter and up to the following year's run. For Renee and I, about twenty-five fish a piece was the magic number. A good day of gill netting could capture all the fish you needed, but I preferred to use a fly rod, just to prolong the enjoyment of it all.

Moving back to Hawaii, I looked with pride into our large chest freezer in the garage, filled with color-coded shopping bags containing nearly every species available offshore: tuna, marlin, mahi-mahi, and ono. It was a fun challenge to keep it properly stocked, as these proteins were the backbone of our weekly meals. They became part of us. I am fond of telling my kids that they are mostly made of fish, as that is what Renee ate while pregnant with them and was among their most common meals as toddlers.

Why Bother?

Why spend your free time and money chasing your food around when you could just as easily pick up some fresh fish steaks at any number of grocery stores? Fair question. I'll call it a primordial force that gets me up at 3 A.M. to catch the incoming tide when the rest of my buddies are just getting home from the bar. But if you're looking for something more to get your head and maybe wallet around, here are some other motivators:

Health: Assuming you are not fishing near a superfund site, there are few things more pure than consuming wild protein. Whether a fish or a lowly crab, these animals have never been fed processed foods, or injected with antibiotics, or had their genetics tinkered with to produce a certain trait. Think about the amount of money we spend on grass-fed beef, having our domesticated animals mimic a wild animal's diet, and then tout its healthiness as reason enough for its exorbitant price. Same goes for buying foods on the basis of the humane nature in which it was raised, like cage-free chickens. But I say, why buy that which mimics nature when we can go straight to the source?

Cost: This is a tricky one depending on where you fish or hunt and how well versed you are. However, I can unequivocally state that in many situations, it is just a much better value. The easy example would be living in Alaska and loading up with halibut and salmon until my freezer was full. The market price of these fish hovered upward of thirty dollars per pound, and I caught enough of them to come out way in the black. But you don't have to go to Alaska to bank a bounty. A sixty-five-dollar ticket on a New England head boat to fish for a full day targeting cod, pollock, and haddock could be money well spent. On most of these trips I brought enough fillets home to enjoy that catch for many meals. In the case of wild game, I could make the argument that the meat is actually priceless. Commercial hunting has been banned for well over one hundred years, and therefore, you could not even find or enjoy elk or mountain goat unless you harvested it yourself.

Fulfillment: This one is probably my personal favorite—it just feels good to harvest my own protein. There is intrinsic value to me in gathering my own food to provide for my family. Call it an ancestral connection, or a family tradition, but taking responsibility for your own food feeds both the body and the soul. I distinctly recall the mix of emotions the first time I shot a deer, an amalgam of excitement, remorse, and happiness. Each time I took out a piece to defrost, that cut of meat demanded a certain level of respect. The connection to your food makes it more than just protein; it makes it *your* protein. We all have been guilty of throwing food away that we either don't want or just don't really care to save. I never do that with food that I harvest. Whether it be a sense of guilt to have not used something that I killed or the integrity to the relationship forged to that kill, you don't want to waste any wild-captured food.

During our years in Alaska and Hawaii, Renee and I were pretty much subsistence living with the protein in our meals. We rotated between pelagic fish, salmon, halibut, deer, and the occasional piece of moose or elk. Chicken was about the only thing we bought, and that was just to keep variety in our dinner menus. It was easy to do there; store-bought meat and fish were expensive while getting your own was accessible. However, life is all about balance, and you have to strike one between fishing/hunting and not scaring your neighbors by skinning deer in the front yard. I learned some of those lessons the hard way when life sent me tumbling from my wild wonderland back to the suburbs and the daily grind of modern living. I still strive toward subsistence, even if I can no longer reach my limit for salmon before work in the mornings.

Let's Not Get Crazy Here

I love eating what I have caught but also cannot always break away from the wants and needs of a growing family and a career. Nor do I necessarily want to miss tea parties with my daughter or a date night with my wife. Life is about balance and enjoying the many things that surround us. Dietary and lifestyle strictness, regardless of how highly motivated you may be, can be a struggle. There's no shame in buying fish and meat, but I enjoy making those weekday meals a product of the un-domesticated world when I can.

When I am out in the wild, the noise of the world falls off. A lot of what seemed terribly important turns out not to be. The volume gets turned up on the rest of my life, the parts that will fill my memories. The sound of the sea and the rivers has a way of rising to the top of where your focus should be. For me, it's the realization that spending time knee-deep in a river or on the sea, harvesting wild fish, and sharing it feels right. There is an innate connection to the world beyond the one that we humans created, and I want to maintain that. Fishing has given me a sense of purpose and because of that, nearly everything I do has some primary or secondary reason related to fishing. Being out on the wild waters, standing with friends, family, or just myself in the wind, alongside bears and whales, is intoxicating to me. It has deepened my connection to this beautiful Earth of ours and sent a few new scars and new friends in my direction as well. I will forever be a student of the sea—learning, experimenting, and reliving the mistakes, usually of losing a big fish, over and over.

The Final Cast

The cultural and fishing outposts of New England, Hawaii, and Alaska stand out to me and keep drawing me back, as if trying to tell me something if I would just be quiet and listen. These corners of the country all contain the last bit of wild ocean and uninterrupted bloodlines of cultural connections. To fish waters that Captain Cook explored in Alaska, or troll the waters that King Kamehameha led his warriors over, or even pass over waters that my own mother traveled as an immigrant provide me a context to my own past, both as an individual and as a part of the human race. And this wilderness remains. The landscape has been significantly altered in the past four-hundred years, yet there exists a seemingly limitless horizon to the fishermen, barren of traces of man, lying just miles offshore that has not been dissected into property lots. The United States' exclusive economic zone, which extends 200 miles offshore of our coasts and islands, covers 3.4 million square miles, the largest in the world. This grand endowment of public trust, available to each of us, is the greatest of gifts and invites me to come to terms with my own untamed side as much as I can.

The Modern English language does not lend itself well to intangibles as it is relates to the human spirit and the natural world. A word exists for the alignment of magnetic fields spewed from the mid-Atlantic ridge, but a word to describe the connection I feel to the fish, and the joy it provides me even when I am cold and wet, isn't in the dictionary. It took moving to and living in these places to feel those ancient connections gradually reestablish themselves as I became part of the land-scape and aligned myself with the rhythm of the sea. That rhythm, that connection I feel when knee-deep in a salmon stream or watching the sun rise from the 500-fathom curve off Waianae, is called *"pono"* in Hawaiian and is best described as balance, goodness, or in harmony. Pono is the ebb and flood of the tides, the perfect cast of a fly rod, or the annual migration of salmon up a river that occurs the same week each year. It is the feeling I get when I fish enough to feel invigorated from it, and the satisfaction of coming home, picking up my kids in my arms, and showing them what I brought for dinner.

When you get that life balance right, what does that pono fuel? The Hawaiians would call that your "*mana*." In Inuit, it would be the "*inua*," best defined as the spirit or life force. The ancients believed that everything has it. A fish has it within. A fisherman will feel it often before a successful trip. I first felt it in the early 1990s, the night before my dad and I went out in the Chesapeake Bay and landed a monster striper. The day we hooked that 611-pound marlin, I could feel it, like static electricity in the air before a thunderstorm, until the ratchet of the massive reel signaled the collision of two worlds.

I was in the Kailua library one rainy afternoon and found an old book titled *The Wai'anae Book of Hawaiian Health*. If you're not from Hawaii you might not think much of that title, but if you know a little about Waianae, you might see that title as a paradox. Waianae is, unfortunately, among the most economically disadvantaged parts of Oahu and is filled with fast-food restaurants. But I have fished out of Waianae for a few years now, and what it lacks in curb appeal, it makes up for in authenticity and, in my view, mana. It has not been gentrified or fashioned into another tourist destination. It is real and gritty and full of culture. This book was about a project to return Hawaiians to historical Hawaiian diets—that of fresh fruits, vegetables, like the Taro plant, and fresh fish. There was a part of the book that stood out to me:

> Eating the proper foods is important because life force is present in all foods. Thus, food is life-giving, not only from a nutritional standpoint but also from

a spiritual standpoint as well. Eating food that is closest to its original state would bear the *mana* from *Papa* (earth mother).

Eating wild foods feed not just the body, but the soul as well.

Pono, inua, mana. These were concepts that I had felt but could not describe. They were the concepts I would circle with words in English that failed to meet their mark in trying to describe to others why I spent my days off from work being cold, wet, and sleep-deprived, for a chance at catching a fish, and when I did land one, why I seemed so happy about it for days after. They were there all along, but I had to live them at their place of origin to understand their meaning. The consumption of wild protein in a respectful manner creates a perfect union of that wildness and my own body. It graces me with that life force, that mana, that inua.

I began as just a kid who loved catching croakers off a dock in South Carolina. But like a river, fishing has taken me on a winding but just course through human history, art, culture, and friendship. Fishing keeps me focused. In maritime navigation, a trackline is drawn on the chart and positions are fixed relative to that trackline. Fishing provided me that trackline, something to drive on. I don't know exactly where the destination will be, but as it is said, it is all about the journey. The discipline of dedicating myself to the craft has made me a better man. There are no doubt numerous intangibles that I owe to fishing, but I don't fish to strengthen my character. I fish in order to live a life filled with focus and desire, with the right balance of pono. Our lives are not a dress rehearsal, and none of us know how many casts we have left. But if my last cast happened tomorrow, I think I would look down and smile. Because of fishing, I have lived a full life.

How to Fish
Like a Local

Appendix 1

Becoming a Fisherman

My path to becoming a fisherman was cut the moment I could walk. It's a familial story, passed down to me from my father, whose knowledge of fishing was taught to him by his father. For me, once that initial match was struck, the resulting flame lit the course of my life. I caught my first tuna by age eight, and taught myself to fly-fish by ten. I was running a boat on my own by the time I was in middle school. These skills were all developed by trial and error from decades of being on and in the water. But what if I wanted to start fishing as an adult and didn't have decades to learn? If you are at this stage and, like most adults, don't have an abundance of time or money to devote to becoming a fisherman, there are ways to get the job done nonetheless.

Wild waters abound in many areas, and a ticket to Alaska doesn't need to be your only opportunity to find adventure—although I would still highly recommend it! In the suburbs of Cleveland, Ohio, I have seen steelhead trout migrations that reminded me of Alaska: arm-length fish coming up local rivers by the hundreds—big, mean, and hungry throughout the winter and spring. In San Francisco Bay, I have pursued California halibut and stripers as I drifted in and out of fog banks, trying to avoid being run down by ferries. America is a wild place; you might not have to look all that far to find your wilderness.

While fishing remote, wild waters is a good long-term goal, you have to first be competent on your local waters. Specifically, I would recommend you pick one species to pursue; ideally, one that doesn't require a boat unless you already have one. Whether that fish lives in fresh or saltwater, it doesn't matter. But focus on one local fish, thus simplifying your pursuit. By doing so, it avoids the overwhelming onslaught of options and choices of gear and locations.

Once you've settled on a particular species, it is time to learn everything there is to know about it. You might call it gathering intel if you are in the military, or market research if you work in business. Books, magazines, and websites abound with information, all of which will provide you data to begin establishing a pattern of life for this fish, along with what regional techniques are used to pursue them. Social media will likewise provide real-time intel on catch information, as most fishermen can't resist posting photos of their recent conquest. From all these sources comes some general knowledge of when and where to find your quarry.

From here, you may want to consider purchasing the right gear. While it is tempting to go to a national chain store or look online, to get the best price, remember to play the long game. The knowledge and connections made at a local tackle store are invaluable. Tackle stores do not make money if they provide bad recommendations or sell lures that don't work. A good tackle shop will take the time to work with you and outfit a new angler with the correct gear that will catch fish. Additionally, I have made some great new fishing buddies by meeting like-minded anglers.

Seek to buy the mid-range gear, rods, and reels that will be reliable but not break the bank. The jump from low-priced cheap gear to mid-range gear is exponential. From mid-range gear to high-end is not so extreme. Remember, you are looking for a 1999 Toyota Corolla, not a Ferrari. Seek to purchase a complete outfit: rod, reel, and line. Additionally, add recommended lures and rigs in order to have a few options. Armed with these tools and local knowledge, it is time to begin scouting.

All fish are looking to minimize energy use, maximize food opportunities, and avoid predators in the process. Rarely would a salmon choose a section of a river with the fastest flowing water to lie in, as it would be a waste of precious energy. They would much rather find a seam of water that is slower moving but adjacent to the fast-flowing water. However, where will most fishermen look to cast? You guessed it, as far out as possible, which is usually in the fastest section, when the fish are likely closer to your feet the whole time.

To find a good spot to fish is to visualize the area without water. Using clues from what is seen on navigational charts, the shoreline, and even how the water looks, an angler can start to draw conclusions of what lies under the surface. Regardless of what species I am searching for, when shore fishing I will gravitate toward an area that has the deepest water, closest to shore. Deep water equals safety for a fish and, regardless of size, they will often venture into shallow water only when they feel it is safe, usually dawn, dusk, and night.

The next step is to look for transition areas, those spots where sand turns to rocks, or shallow waters fall off to deep. Those edges represent changes in habitats for various prey, as well as ambush areas. A large predatory fish would prefer to patrol the deep side of a drop-off, which provides security and an escape, while it scans for feed opportunities up in the shallows. I see this at night as well. Artificial lights shining on the surface attract plankton, small crustaceans, and small baitfish. Rather than be exposed in the light, the large predators will remain in the darkness and dash into the light only when a meal option presents itself.

Once prospective areas are found, it is time to go fishing. Regardless of the tide, moon, or many other factors that can affect your chances of catching a fish, simply being at a spot early is one factor that has been crucial for me. After the nighttime reset, the fish are relaxed and undisturbed. Many predatory fish are "crepuscular," meaning that they are most active at dawn and dusk. These times are the change in shifts. After the night shift, those species that are mostly nocturnal become less active at dawn, while the day shift is just ramping up. Additionally, the change in light can be difficult for smaller baitfish compared to larger predators with more capable vision.

Silhouetted against a brightening surface, predators can once again ambush bait close to shore by using deepwater routes to quickly enter into the shallows and retreat before the sun gets too high.

Many of my fishing trips begin at 4 A.M. and are over by 8. If it didn't happen at dawn, there is a good chance it just isn't going to happen. An additional benefit to fishing this early is the lack of impact to the rest of your life. For those with growing families, disappearing for most of the day translates to more work for your spouse. But an early morning—a tactical strike, if you will—is no problem at all. One of my crowning achievements was once getting up to go red salmon fishing in Kodiak around 3 A.M., fishing for several hours, catching my limit of fish, and crawling back into bed before my wife woke up.

I moved to the seacoast of New Hampshire for a few years, an area I had never fished before. I arrived in midsummer, when the striper season was in full swing. I wanted to start catching fish right away, but was faced with the challenge of learning new home waters. By the end of that season, I was routinely catching, having found several good spots to frequent. Here is how I did it.

Upon arriving, I did internet searches on the area and found lists of known fishing spots, taking note of where they were. I then went to my local tackle store to buy a license, pick up some new lures, and talk shop. When the historical fishing spots that I found online came up in conversation with shop owners, things started looking promising. I then scouted the area using navigational charts. Giving myself twenty miles of coastline to scan, I marked the areas of the coast that came up in conversation, as well as new spots that had any unusual geographic features, which would be potential ambush points. Likewise, I took note if any of these areas had drop-offs nearby. The spot with the deepest water closest to the shore moved to the top of my list. Now it was time to check it out in person. I could find the best spot in the world, but if it was located on private property, it wouldn't do me much good. Likewise, parking is a challenge that can make or break a good fishing spot. These scouting trips are also a good time to bring kids along. It's fun to walk the shoreline or jump around on the rocks, looking for adventure and small sea creatures.

Most importantly, the location now becomes "our spot." The one we selected on one of the scouting trips with my kids was a rocky point that transitioned to a sandy beach nearby. The rocks were relatively high and suggested that the water dropped off quickly. Another sign I liked was the proximity of lobster buoys. This told me that the bottom was rocky, held a food source, and was deep enough for lobster boats to get into—all good signs.

With the homework done, it was time to get out there. When chasing stripers, I like to arrive at the spot early enough to need to wear a headlamp. After a long sip of coffee in my 4Runner before my first trip out to my spot, I stepped off and began working my way through the rocks. It is always surprising how different a spot looks in the dark, so it is best to take your time. A key point for low-light fishing is to take care not to shine any lights on the water. This is a quick way of alerting any nearby stripers of human presence, so I either use red lights or take care that the light doesn't reach the water.

My first trip to my new spot yielded a schoolie striper, not big enough to keep, yet enough to let me know that I picked a winner of a location. Noting the tide, moon, time, and lure used, I could start patterning the trends I was finding. I kept adding to my list of spots by forcing myself to fish new areas using the same criteria I used with the first one. Once I found a few proven spots, persistence was the key. I knew fish frequented these spots, and would fish them either early in the morning or later in the evening after I put my kids to bed. Keeping a consistent pulse on the spots, I knew that the full moon incoming tide was productive and I would seek to be there when those occurred. The fish were there, and we enjoyed some wonderful striper dinners as a result.

To accelerate your learning, seek out any of the numerous local guides that assist anglers of all skill levels. While some new anglers may enjoy the DIY aspect of figuring out local waters, others do not have the time to dedicate to slowly moving up the learning curve. A way around this is to hire a guide or an outfitter. Guide services can be as simple as a person who will take you to local trout spots on a river to as complicated as hiring a charter boat that might supply everything needed but food. Of course, this comes with a price—typically, a high price. But this is a great way of unveiling the mystery of local fishing. I don't know of any guide who wouldn't enjoy downloading all the knowledge they can into an eager fisherman, especially to a new angler. A good technique would be to go with a guide first to get your sea legs on a particular fishery and hopefully have some early success. With early success, an angler's confidence grows, and going out on their own for the next trip seems far less daunting with that experience under one's belt.

A lower priced option than going with a charter boat is to jump on a head boat, or party boat. Rather than chartering the entire boat, you pay by the "head," thus the term head boat. For reasonable prices, this gets you offshore and into some fish. The tradeoff is that you are one of many anglers, which reduces the amount of teaching you get, while increasing your likelihood of tangles. But they are a great option for getting out on the water. Even with my years of running boats, I appreciate the simplicity of not worrying about anything except showing up on time. In areas like New England, fishing head boats allow anglers to fish later in the season and often in weather that would be a show-stopper for a smaller boat.

Perhaps the biggest takeaway when either scouting out new waters or just becoming a fisherman is to be patient. Beginner's luck is a rare event and most things in life need to be earned. Learning is an incremental process and fishing often feels like correctly placing puzzle pieces through multiple trips until success is found. If you are starting out fishing as an adult, there is a reason why you felt the need. It might be to seek peace, procure your own food, or take on a new life skill. Regardless of the motivation, keeping an open mind, being humble, and practicing patience are key.

Appendix: 2

Fly-Fishing

I cannot recall anyone who began their fishing career by jumping right into fly-fishing. It's akin to learning how to play ice hockey: It's best to take up the sport only after becoming competent at ice-skating. I recommend having a firm grasp on how to fish before moving into the advanced aspects of it. Fly-fishing involves using a heavier line, called a fly line, to propel a comparatively weightless lure, called a fly, out into the water. Doing so without the momentum of the fly line would be nearly impossible. The fly, tied with fur, feathers, and hair, can precisely mimic anything from the tiniest mosquito to a large baitfish. The fly line itself can float, sink, or just sink at the front, which is called a "sink tip." On the reel behind the fly line is what is called "backing." This is either a dacron or braided line that provides an extra reservoir of line should a large fish take to a long run. When fighting a big fish, an angler will often say "it took me into the backing," implying the fish took a long run and took all the fly line out. While often associated with trout fishing because of the very specific aquatic insects that inhabit a stream, nearly every species can be targeted using a fly rod, from the largest marlin down to a sunfish in a local pond.

Fly rods are graded out based on weight. The smallest and lightest fly rods available are two- or three-weight rods, designed to pursue fish in small creeks with tiny flies, perhaps a tiny brook trout creek in Maine or a North Carolina mountain stream that requires a very precise cast among the trees. On the other end of the spectrum is a fifteen-weight fly rod that would be used to target the largest marlin or tuna you dared to tangle with. These rods are capable of throwing large, heavy flies as far as possible, usually behind a boat toward a big fish. Most of a fly fisherman's time is spent between these two. Regardless of the weight, every fly rod is designed to flex and bow. As a back cast is taken and the rod is pushed forward, the slingshot motion of the rod—that energy being released—is what moves the fly line. The downside of fly rods is that they lack a lot of backbone. While an angler can really lean back against a spinning or conventional rod should he or she need to pressure a fish, fly rods, often over eight feet long and wispy, do not apply that much pressure. It is the fun part of it, and at times the frustrating part of it, as the fish will often go where it wants.

Starting off, a great rod choice is a six- or seven-weight rod with floating line. Like the Goldilocks concept, this outfit is light enough for most any trout or freshwater fishing situation, while also being capable enough to tangle with a moderate sized fish like bass or salmon, should you dare. I fished with just this one size for most of my life until I moved to Alaska and realized I was under-equipped for daily battles with big salmon.

Alaska has a certain way of not so subtly making you buy good gear. My first salmon season I broke six rods. The first three were seven-weight rods and the remaining were eight-weights. It was impressively depressing, but the reds and silvers were big and I also didn't have the patience to properly land a pink. There are two reasons for this: First, after inadvertently hooking yet another "zombie" pink, my natural inclination was to quickly get the fish in. But these fish have a lot of fight and will literally battle to the death. Second, once beached, pinks do not stop flopping. This will either cause me to "high stick" or allow the fish to get back into the river and make a quick getaway. Either way is bad news for a wispy fly rod. Be patient and land the fish, it is cheaper.

Additionally, if I wasn't breaking rods, I found myself a few times hooking into salmon that took off downstream and left me hanging on. In several instances, the fish actually left the river and headed back out to sea. At the mouth of most rivers are hungry seals trying to grab migrating salmon, and I can remember the crushing feeling of a seal grabbing hold of my salmon and ripping it away. The speed at which the line began to peel off the reel before my hook pulled out was frightening,

I would have likely lost all my fly line and backing in seconds. More firepower was needed.

The day I broke rod number six, I walked into the tackle shop with my waders on, looking for something better. I went with a nine-weight Sage TCX and haven't looked back. It was a steep initial cost, and I was close to dry heaving in the parking lot after purchasing it. The rod has more than paid for itself by landing several hundred salmon flawlessly. My reel choice is a Ross, CLA 5. It isn't a flashy reel but it's a workhorse, and Ross stands behind their craftsmanship. Spooled with floating line and spectra backing, it is ready for all five salmon species. At first glance, a nine-weight might seem a little heavy, but I can't recall one trip in which I thought that was the case. Bottom line is, it just doesn't break like the other ones. For all my salmon fishing, I rely exclusively on this combination and haven't felt the need to use anything else. This single combination has landed hundreds of salmon and is the right balance of being able to throw heavy flies and to turn a salmon before it gets out to the seal band saw, while still not being overkill.

At the end of the fly line, a monofilament leader connects the bulky fly line to the fly. In classic fly-fishing, this "leader" which ranges in length from six to fifteen feet, is tapered as it decreases in diameter toward the fly, to help the fly more naturally roll out as it is casted, the last bit of the leader is called the "tippet." But these tapered leaders are not cheap and, at least for an Alaskan fly-fisherman, are not as necessary. At the end of my fly line, I tie an Albright knot to a ten-inch piece of forty-pound test monofilament. I then tie a small perfection loop in the monofilament. This loop serves as my connection for all my other leaders and will practically last all season. In my shoulder sling tackle box, I carry a bag of twelve-foot, ten-pound test leaders, each with a perfection loop at the end. Using a loop-to-loop, or "cat's paw," connection, I can quickly switch out leaders as they either break or become chafed throughout the day. Some days, if fishing is good, I might tear through three or four leaders. The panic of seeing a large school of salmon in front of you requires a fast turnaround time for re-tying, so having a bag full of leaders ready to go is the quickest way to do it.

Like any pursuit, fly-fishing comes with its own assumptions about the end user. Comments ranging from "out-of-touch" elitists to stubbornness has been directed toward fly fishermen. What makes non-fly fishermen suspicious are their misconceived notions that these anglers think they can replace knowledge with a fly vest full of assorted gear and gadgetry, armed with a holier-than-thou attitude. As someone who straddles the fly-fishing and conventional world, I have a little different take on it.

Although the primary reason I like to put down a conventional or spinning reel and pick up a fly rod is because I think I will catch more fish doing so, the other reason is that it feels like a thing of beauty. There is an art form to fly casting. I have no musical or dancing talent, but due to fly-fishing, I know I have rhythm. While a conventional cast involves just one quick snap of the rod forward to cast out a weighted lure, fly-fishing, especially for a cast of distance, requires the angler to draw back the line behind them and suspend it in the air as it unravels like a bull whip. Before it falls, it is swept forward and again, held in the air momentarily. Too fast and the line will tangle with itself and fall, creating knots in the line in the process. Too slow and it will fall from the sky and snag the ground. But to make a perfect cast with a fly rod is to feel in tune with the world. Correctly done, the line will shoot from the guides of the rod effortlessly with just the swoosh of the line being heard as it falls like a feather onto the water. It is beauty in motion when done correctly, and is a relaxing way of spending a day.

I have had days where I know I will likely not catch anything but went anyway, just to experience the joy of it all, casting my fly rod. When the fish does strike, the rod is pulled, and the fly line comes ripping off the water's surface with a noise that most reminds me of tape being pulled off a wall. With extra fly line in the water, a fisherman has to simultaneously keep pressure on the fish while reeling as fast as one can with the other hand to get the excess line back on the reel. Except for the most expensive ones, most fly reels will spin backward as the fish runs; failure to let go of the handle will quickly break the line. Likewise, the reels are slow, and when a feisty salmon changes direction and starts running toward you, you cannot recover line fast enough. I have been known to sprint upstream in waders to keep the line taunt. The long, wispy rods are always at risk of breaking and many of my rods have met their demise on the banks of the river with a fish on the other end.

But looking through my logbook, it is clear that by far, fly-fishing is my most productive way of catching salmon. Many times, it is the only effective way to present a lure to a fish without spooking it. Most salmon I catch on a fly rod are seen first. Moving up clear, shallow rivers, anything but a nearly weightless, delicate cast would spook them back out to sea. I have found myself crawling up to a riverbank to stalk resting salmon in water that barely covers them. Working myself into a reasonable casting distance far from the river's edge, I gracefully release a cast upstream of the fish. The subtle drop of the fly, well ahead of the fish does not bother them much, and as a result the fly drifts into their field of vision and is quickly snatched. It is a spectacular sight to see and a deeply rewarding experience.

To be a proficient fly fisherman is to round out one's skill in angling. It may not be the predominant way you fish, but there are times when it is the only thing that will work. Beyond that, the joy of feeling the rhythm of the rod is the perfect way to slow down and unwind from life's stresses.

Appendix 3

New England

Stripers

I call my surf casting rod the "OTH," the Over the Horizon, as due to its size, it can send a lure far into the distance. Made by Penn, it's a full twelve feet long. My reel is also made by Penn and likely exists in more than a few anglers' antique collections. The Penn reel was likely made over thirty years ago and lacks about anything that would attract a modern angler to a reel. I bought it used when I was thirteen, and it probably was created around the time that Reagan was president. What it lacks in curb appeal, it makes up for in its amazingly simple engineering that allows me to submerge it in saltwater without consequence. My affinity for this reel could also be my tip of the cap to the old-school roots of the technique. I spool my trusty reel with comparatively light, Ande monofilament twenty-pound line, which is a bit harder than other brands so it holds up better to abrasion. With lighter line, I can really zip a plug offshore. One other trick I like to do is to fill the bottom half of the spool with braided line. This way I can pack more line on the arbor, in the event that I hook a bigger fish, and I can swap out the monofilament "top shot" without losing hundreds of yards of line. This twenty-pound main line ends with a Binimi twist that connects to a four-foot section of fifty-pound test leader via a Bristol knot and ends with a snap.

Lure choices are the fun part. Steeped in tradition, throwing wooden plugs seems fitting when working this iconic New England fishery. There are generally three types of wooden plugs that I throw: poppers, pencil poppers, and swimmers. Poppers are generally a flat or concave-faced surface lure, designed to throw spray and cause commotion. They are the preferred choice when bluefish are present, or when fish are "blitzing," or breaking the surface and feeding. Essentially, if you want to make some noise, poppers are your lure. Pencil poppers are a bit more refined. They are the gentlemanly option to the marauding poppers. I always pictured stripers as a more gentlemanly fish anyway. Rather than blast the surface and cause chaos, the rear weights partially submerge the lure, causing the front to slap the water. They are also useful because I can cover a lot of water with them to find where the fish might be when casting. If I raise a fish but it misses, after a few casts I will switch to a swimmer.

Danny swimmers look like a popper with a metal lip, and when reeled slowly, they lazily wobble on the surface. When used on calm water, often in low light, they are a magnet for big stripers. They can't be cast as far, nor do they always make it out of the bag, but when conditions are right, stand by.

Beyond the classic wooden lures are multiple other options. Every striper fisherman will carry bucktails. These are weighted jigs with deer hair tied to the back and come in every size and color imaginable. For surf casting, I will have a few one-to-two-ounce bucktails with me most of the time, in either white or chartreuse colors. Bucktails' success is maximized when they are fished with a trailer. This is a small attractor attached to the hook that dangles beyond the bucktail, most closely resembling a tail. Plastic twister tails are often the most popular, with again, chartreuse as my favorite color. Bucktails are easy to fish: simply cast out and slowly retrieve while lifting the rod. The up and down motion resembles a squid or oblivious baitfish swimming through the water and is easy pickings for a nearby striper.

Another lure I will keep with me is the Bomber Long A. It is known as a stick bait and, with a plastic lip, will dive underwater and seductively wiggle as it is retrieved. These lures are simple, affordable, and deadly. The Long A comes in a jointed (think hinge in the middle) and non-jointed model. I think the jointed one is the most effective, but it cannot be cast as far. My go-to color is white for most applications, but black is proven to be good at night, as it creates a silhouette against the surface. Keep one in your box; you won't be disappointed.

When in doubt, particularly at night, live eels are the ticket to some of the biggest stripers. Locally purchased at many bait shops, they can also be trapped in local marshes and streams. Eels are a hardy bait that can be cast many times. With no weight and just a single hook, a slow retrieve is the prefect technique. Strikes are not like a hammer but rather a bump and then a steady pressure. If fishing at night, give a live eel a cast.

Surf Casting Gear

I pack light when surf casting and carry just what I need for a trip. From head to toe, I am particular in what I carry with me. Except in rare circumstances, I seem to always wear a water-resistant jacket. It blocks the wind, rain, and sea spray. In its pocket I keep a headlamp. I will normally be going in while it's dark or coming out after dark. All my fishing gear fits into an Orvis shoulder sling tackle box. Key contents include: pliers with line cutters, extra leader, roughly six lures, and a measuring tape. Large wooden plugs tangle with themselves and around everything else in a nylon bag. To circumvent this, I cut the tops off of clear plastic water bottles. Into each bottle goes one or two lures, making them easy to retrieve in the dark.

On my waist I wear an elastic belt with an incredibly sharp dive knife attached. Whether I need to dispatch a fish, cut tangled line, or worst-case scenario, cut myself free if I become tangled in something, carrying a knife is a good idea.

My pants of choice are more toward hiking pants, with a nice blend of stretch and comfort. For shoes, I almost always choose Xtratuf boots, which I will occasionally flood, but the calf-high top usually keeps me out of trouble. One final addition are ice cleats. Slipping on rocks is second to being swept off by a large wave in terms of biggest dangers when surf casting. With ice cleats, I can hop from rock to rock with confidence. They are easy to slip on or off and, when not in use, reside on a carabineer clip on my pack. All these specific choices represent a functional system geared toward success.

Where To Go

Finding new spots may seem daunting, but there are clues to cut down on the guesswork. When I begin fishing a new area, I like to study its nautical chart. This provides immediate clues as to what fish will key into. First, I scan for the deepest water, closest to shore. Shallow water is threatening to big stripers and they will generally only come into the shallows after dark. Proximity to deep water gives an easy escape point, and just as important, an ambush point for passing feed.

My next clues are points of land, ideally jutting out into deep water. A point disrupts the tidal currents, conserving the striper's energy while it watches for passing bait. The change in depth creates a rip by forcing water up toward the surface. This is a tough thing to navigate if you are a herring or mackerel, making them vulnerable to the powerful striper with its big, square tail.

The final clue I look for is rocks. Stripers love rocky areas, which makes sense for a species known as a rockfish. There is more food present near a rocky bottom than a typical sandy bottom. When I find a rocky point jutting out into deep water, I know there will be fish there sooner or later. Now it is time to start fishing it. I will generally start just before sunrise, working all parts of the area, while noting the tide. For reasons still unclear to me, certain spots best produce at certain tides. This is why keeping a fishing log is important to document these small details and pick up on patterns.

One last point on finding new spots: If you ever come across a stretch of shoreline named after fish, it is worth checking out. New Englanders are an upfront people, so if it's called "Striper Beach," you can bet someone has caught some fish there in the past.

Cod Fishing

The more I cod fished, the lighter the tackle I used. Traditional New England tackle is a Penn Senator 4/0 reel and an eight-foot broomstick of a rod. Holding that outfit all day starts to wear on you, so you end up resting on the gunwale of the boat, and that is when you get a big bite and miss it. So, I like to scale down to something I can hold comfortably all day. This is a seven-foot medium action Shimano rod with an Avet LX reel, with sixty-five-pound test Jerry Brown braided line. With this outfit, I can work a fourteen-ounce jig or bottom fish without it wearing me out.

The big decision for each of my cod-fishing trips is deciding if I want to work a jig or fish bait. I will be overt in saying that I much prefer to jig; it feels as if I am an active participant in fishing and big cod have a soft spot for jigs. Realistically, however, if you are fishing south of Cape Cod, at least start with bait. For me, the cod farther south don't respond as well to jigs. I have basically three categories of cod jigs. Norwegian jigs: these are shaped loosely like a banana and when yo-yo jigged have a distinct flutter to them. I would consider these to be my standby choice. Diamond jigs: these are shaped like a cigar with four flat sides. They have less action than a Norwegian and are best reeled up slowly, then dropped back to the bottom. Finally, butterfly jigs: made by Shimano, these new jigs have reflective and glow-in-the-dark sides, with hooks at the top of the lure called "assist hooks." They fish more like a Norwegian jig and catch a lot of fish. Regulations allow for two hooks per line. This means that when jigging, I always put a "teaser" eighteen to twenty-four inches above the jig. This can be anything from a rubber shrimp to a generic hair fly. When jigged, it appears that the jig is chasing the smaller teaser and will often result in double hook ups.

Bait fishing is more straightforward. The iconic bait is fresh clams, a scent that will remain on your clothes and gear for weeks to come. Always bring a rag, your car seats will appreciate it. But fresh shrimp, mackerel, or squid also works. Bring several choices to see what is preferred that day. Like anything, fresh is the best. Bait is fished on a "hi-low" rig, which places one piece of bait close to the bottom, while the second piece is about three feet up. On the top hook, I like to place a teaser, with my favorite being a chartreuse Berkley gulp grub. I slide the grub up to the eye of the hook. The addition of the grub adds a little more eye candy to the rig and the impregnated scent seems to draw in more fish.

Locations

Cod are consistently caught as far south as New Jersey and up to the Canadian border. On much of their southern range, the preferred times to target cod are late fall through the spring. Between these off-season times and the often-challenging weather that goes along with them, most fishing is done from head boats and charter boats. The good news with these is that the geographic locations are taken care of; all you have to pick is your spot on the boat, which can actually matter. The most popular spots are the two back corners, the stern, and then the bow. The sides are the least preferred spots and often only inexperienced fishermen will knowingly choose to fish here.

There are a couple reasons for this. First, cod fishing is often done at anchor. The fish finder transducer, which emits the sonar, is often located on the stern of the boat. This means that the captain is positioning the boat based on the view from the stern and the bow could be off the structure that is holding the fish.

Second, dropping numerous baits at once creates an impressive chum slick behind the boat. Like walking past a bakery with fresh cookies, any fish who crosses that scent trail will follow it to the source. Which baited hooks will they encounter first? You guessed it, the anglers on the stern. Finally, there are generally less tangles on the stern as anglers can underhand cast their rigs away from the boat. Less tangles means more time that your hook is on the bottom.

Farther north, and particularly north of Cape Cod, cod become more of a year-round fishery and are well within reach of private boat owners. To pursue cod, and their cousins haddock and pollock, means to find structure, usually in the form of banks, ledges, and wrecks. Famous fishing banks like Stellwagen, Tillies, Wildcat Knoll, and Jeffreys Ledge have been hot spots for hundreds of years. Beginning at the shallowest depth, I will typically drift fish if possible and determine if the fish are on to shallow top or along the drop offs.

Once the fish density is found, I focus just on these spots and even anchor if it's that good. Going back to the great bait versus jigs debate, I like to drift fish with jigs and switch to bait once anchored up. For a bait rig to fish properly, it should be on the bottom. However, dragging rigs across the bottom causes numerous snags and are also unnatural looking. A fluttering jig, just above the seabed, is a better exploratory option in my opinion.

Bluefin Tuna Fishing

Bluefin tuna fishing is the apex of angling. The gear requirements for fishing bluefin in New England are very similar to those required in Hawaii, and I consider the two interchangeable. Like bare-knuckle boxing and marriage, there is no dipping your toe into bluefin fishing, it has to be all or nothing. To pursue bluefins seriously off of a private boat requires extensive rigging. Rod holders need to be re-enforced to withstand the force of battling the fish. A harpoon is also a smart investment to tame unruly fish. Getting a larger fish into the boat is a chore and some anglers will carry block and tackles to provide a mechanical advantage. To stow even smaller-size fish requires a thermal fish bag or larger cooler capable of carrying several hundred pounds of ice if needed to properly cool down the fish. Seeking tuna more than occasionally is a commitment and a significant financial investment as well. But it is also a fish that you can easily become obsessed with and that can cause you to solely focus on its pursuit.

It is a highly regulated fishery and only fish of a certain size are allowed to be retained for recreational fishing. The size limits change but it is safe to say that the smaller fish are kept by recreational fishermen, while the larger fish, some weighing over a thousand pounds, usually require a commercial license. Those larger fish are generally caught utilizing a technique called "chunking," in which cut bait is used from an anchored boat. The smaller fish are pursued more by trolling or casting. The key for this fishery is taking the time to properly invest in the right gear. There are several tackle stores that sell solid used gear. In the northeast, J&B Tackle in Niantic, Connecticut, is a store that comes to mind. Once you acquire the correct gear, there are a few regional distinctions in chasing bluefin.

The standard trolling lure for bluefin is a spreader bar. This resembles a very large coat hanger with up to a dozen large rubber bulb squid hanging from it. However, only the last squid has a hook in it. Using a bit of fish psychology, the last squid is positioned noticeably farther away from his mates, and is almost always a different color and larger. This singles it out and nearly every strike will be to this outermost bait. Black is the go-to color but bright pink is also popular. Unlike Hawaiian trolling, these are generally pulled at slower speeds, with five knots being average.

A second lure that has gained a lot of traction is a sluggo. This was the lure I used to hook the fish that nearly cost me my hand. A sluggo is a freshwater bass lure, and is nothing more than a slender piece of supple rubber. However, it is a dead ringer for a sand eel imitation when trolled. The standard set-up is to run a medium-sized Owner Jobu hook down the middle of the sluggo, exiting the body at the halfway point. Then a one-ounce egg sinker is slid down the hundred-pound leader to the lay against the sluggo. When trolled slowly at three knots, the sluggo's tail whips naturally and fools a lot of fish. I have also used this same technique in Hawaii for big mahi-mahi.

If you can find them, trolling rigged ballyhoo is fantastic tuna bait as well. Ballyhoo is a small, silver baitfish roughly the size of a herring. They are present in warmer waters, with Florida being the predominant location for commercially sourced baits. The wonderful trait about ballyhoo is how well they can be trolled. Properly defrosted, ballyhoo can be trolled at speeds close to eight knots without tearing off the hook. Typically rigged with a single hook protruding from the belly and a small egg sinker under its chin for ballast, they swim just as good dead as they do alive. Being and smelling real, it is hard for a tuna to pass up ballyhoo and, wherever I troll, from Hawaii to Massachusetts, I will look to use ballyhoo whenever I can.

Particularly south of Cape Cod, I have had good success with running Hawaiian-style lures. A five-inch Matsu (Hawaiian-made resin head), rigged on 150-pound test leader has been a very effective bait for me. Running that on a rig at the typical Hawaiian speed of seven to nine knots has caused many smaller bluefin (under fifty pounds) to pounce.

Beyond trolling, a secondary method of pursuing bluefin is to cast to them with heavy spinning tackle. Finding bird piles, anglers will drive up to a crashing tuna school to cast lures into the mix. With the sizes of these fish extending up to the hundreds of pounds, the spinning tackle is oversize; I would recommend the Shimano Stella and Van Staal spinning reels. This option is good for anglers who may not be targeting tuna, but should fish be sighted, can shift gears and potentially hook up with one.

Locations for bluefin begin in the far reaches of Maine and extend the entire length of the eastern seaboard and even into the Gulf of Mexico, with centralized hot spots being Massachusetts, Long Island, and North Carolina. Bluefins have two recognized spawning stocks: one that spawns in the Mediterranean Sea and swims across the Atlantic to feed, and another stock that spawns in the Gulf of Mexico and also feeds along the eastern seaboard. For New England, Father's Day is often the unofficial start to the season, with earlier catches sometimes happening in the mid-Atlantic states. The fish continue to move north and will be in Maine's waters by midsummer. They remain in the area longer than people think, with catches well into November being routine. There is also a winter fishery off North Carolina during the midwinter months, as the species backtracks down the coast.

Bluefins are notorious for being everywhere and nowhere all at the same time. Known spots like Stellwagen Bank south of Gloucester, the Regal Sword wreck east of Cape Cod, and the mud hole off Block Island are areas that are known to consistently produce. But they also will pop up inshore. I was once pursuing bluefish along the rocks of Gloucester when a tuna roughly the size of a small car came crashing out of the water, pursuing the same bluefish. They are not intimidated by shallow water and it's always a great surprise to fishermen when they hit lures not intended for them.

Alaska

Ocean Salmon Fishing

S almon fishing, while the fish are still in the open ocean, is divided into two main categories: trolling and mooching. Trolling is the most widely accepted method of salmon fishing, particularly when targeting king salmon. Unlike tuna fishing, the speed for salmon fishing is dead slow, usually one to two knots, with the use of downriggers, which position the bait or lure at a certain depth by use of a heavy cannon ball that could weigh up to 20 pounds. With the exception of silver salmon, most salmon species stay deep, often fifty to one hundred feet, and suspended off the bottom.

Trolling with your lure or bait constantly in this strike zone is the overall best way to achieve success. It can be monotonous on slow days, but seeing the line release from the downrigger clip then double-over on a heavy fish is something that will make your heart race like nothing else. It might turn out to be just a pink salmon, but it could be that next hundred-pound white king.

Trolling outfits for salmon usually consist of long, wispy trolling rods with small conventional reels. Typically, long rods are not favored for any boat application but the thought process with the long rods is that the rod will rapidly take up the slack from the main line as the fish strikes, setting the hook in the process. However, I am not convinced that actually occurs, and I have gotten away from using them because they are a hassle in almost any size boat. Even with braided line, which has zero stretch, when trolling at depths over fifty feet, the line has a significant bend or belly in it that cannot be taken out. Once the fish hits, the downrigger release is what causes the hook to be set, and the forward motion of the boat quickly takes the slack out, while the flasher provides constant tension. In my opinion, the rod, which at most will recoil three feet, doesn't play a significant role in the process, except for alerting the angler of a strike.

Once a salmon is hooked, a long rod is an immediate disadvantage; anyone who has trolled before has struggled to close the final gap between a salmon and the net by pulling the rod high into the air, which is an easy way of breaking it. A shorter rod brings the arch of the rod back toward the angler and provides more lift capability as well as ease of handling in a tight cockpit. What a longer rod does contribute is shock absorption; most modern rods have a good balance of flexibility and backbone. My favorite trolling rod is a seven-foot Shimano Trevala. It is the same rod that I have caught cod with off New England, and even big halibut with it on Kodiak. It has a fair amount of parabolic arch, but has enough backbone to put the screws to a big salmon when you are trying to lift it. Shorter rods are easier on the angler and make landing fish easier as well.

Lure Choices

There is an incredible amount of salmon lure choices out there, and they all work. Walking through a tackle store in Alaska, it is impressive to see the selection of lure colors. But to distill it down, there are spoons, hootchies, Ace Hi Flys, plugs, and bait. Each of these baits can be trolled behind a "flasher" or "dodger." Before your mind wanders too far, a flasher in salmon terms is a piece of metal or plastic, slightly smaller than a car's license plate that is positioned about two feet ahead of a trolled lure. It darts and "flashes" down in the water, drawing attention to the lure behind it, while also causing the lure to have the same erratic action. Hats off to the first fisherman who figured this out, as they are very effective in drawing fish to your spread.

Trolling spoons are nearly weightless pieces of teardrop-shaped metal, usually ranging from three to six inches in length. But with their lack of weight, they are able to flutter beautifully as they are trolled. Many commercial trollers will rely on spoons to make a substantial portion of their catch and therefore have a home in most troller's tackle boxes.

Hootchies, or squid skirts, are just that—a miniaturized version of the skirts, which, in Hawaii, are tied to resin head lures. They are trolled behind a flasher, which makes them dance, and are a popular choice for trolling. I personally have not had a ton of success with them, but they do produce.

Ace Hi Flys are lures with a synthetic skirt and a small plastic head, similar to a Hawaiian-style resin head. They are nearly weightless and, like a hootchie, have no intrinsic action. But they are my favorite. When trolling, I will always have an Ace Hi out and in the mix.

Salmon plugs are an old-school lure for trolling. With a tapered body and angled face, they produce an erratic action when trolled behind a downrigger and are also a favorite of commercial trollers and generally old school anglers. I do not have a lot of experience with them personally, but they do work.

The final option is to troll bait. Using the real deal is always a good idea, but it is harder. Herring are tougher to keep on the hook and require constant checking to ensure they have not been stripped off the hook or are not fishing properly. But if you have the patience, they will produce fish.

Salmon don't have big teeth, but they are sharp enough to chafe through leaders. Renee and I experienced this one day while out trolling with my friend Jim Morrow. It was a frustrating day. After a slow morning, we found a pile of salmon around 3 P.M. Jim was at the wheel and, being a C-130 airplane pilot, would announce, "We are on our short final," every time we were about to pass over the area holding the fish. Sure enough, the short final would result in at least a knock down but for some reason, I couldn't keep the fish from cutting through our store-bought leaders. The violent head shaking near the boat was enough to cut through the line; it was frustrating. We came home with a small king and a silver, but had lost many more. Nearly every fish we lost had cut the thirty-pound test leader directly in front of the hook.

Searching for a solution, I reached into my tuna fishing tackle box for a special type of defense: chafing tube—clear, hard tubing that is routinely used between the hook and a lure to prevent offshore species from cutting the line. When paired with forty-pound fluorocarbon leader, it provides the perfect answer to getting chafed off by kings. I began tying my own leaders and put a two-inch length of chafing tube between the front and back hook of those leaders, which was almost imperceptible in the skirt of an Ace Hi.

Later that season, I hooked and landed my biggest king to date, that beautiful thirty-pound fish that I described earlier. It fell for my trusty Ace Hi. The rear hook is what the fish hit, and the chafing tube, which was centered along the bottom teeth, showed plenty of scrape marks, but the fluorocarbon leader was untouched.

When trolling I also like to keep the boat slowly moving forward after a fish is hooked. This technique of staying clutched-in (meaning that you leave the boat in gear, slowly moving forward) or at least bumping ahead, keeps the fish behind the boat and keeps the line tight. Slack in the line is what causes most fish to be lost, and with the salmon so deep, it is imperative to be mindful of it. Additionally, it can lead to double hook-ups, as salmon are a schooling fish and others will pounce on the remaining lures. As a salmon is reeled toward the boat: letting a fish get ahead of the boat or under it is bad news. The boat is the only cover in open water and a smart fish will use it to its advantage. This technique pairs very well with tip number one, using a shorter rod with more backbone, as the additional drag added from the forward movement of the boat is tough to manage with a long, wimpy rod, which is maybe why it isn't often used. One other tip: as the salmon approaches the boat, have the helmsman slowly turn toward the side of the boat the angler is on. This keeps the fish away from the engine, shortens the distance between the net and the fish, and puts the fish on a perfect angle to be slid into the net.

Silver salmon are not so focused as king salmon are on staying deep, and will wander all through the water column. They can often be seen jumping on the surface. Once the silvers begin to arrive in July and August, I like to run a flat line (also called a "shotgun" in Hawaii). To cover all the bases, I attach a two- to three-ounce torpedo sinker about four feet in front of a spoon and send it way back. If your boat has "rocket launchers" (rod holders on the pilot house), this is a perfect time to use them, because the rod will stay out of your way and you might not even notice it until it doubles over. We had one trip where the silvers were in shallow water as they prepared to run up a river. At forty feet deep, we lowered the downriggers just barely out of sight, maybe fifteen feet below the surface.

The proximity to the boat didn't matter and the salmon readily attacked our lures. Our limits were quickly filled.

When running hootchies, Ace His, or other skirted lures, I like to add a little fillet of herring or anchovy to the front hook, extending to the eye of the rear hook. Why the front hook? Because I want the fish to attack the area of the lure that has the hooks, rather than on the rear hook, which could result in a missed fish. I often bring herring for mooching. It's a great use of bait that may have thawed out and won't be refrozen. It's not much, but it adds some scent to the lure. I have caught plenty of fish without any added scent, but on those days where the fish are tough to find, I think it helps convince the wary ones to strike.

Watching a rod pop up and then double over while trolling is a sight that will make your heart skip a beat. Salmon trolling often feels like a combination of choreographed dancing with a healthy splash of witchcraft as the smallest details sometimes separate success from failure. But it is a really fun and effective way to pursue salmon before they reach the river. If you happen to find a big pile of salmon, it might be time to stop the boat and mooch.

To "mooch" is to fish with small herring. Mooching involves slowly retrieving plug-cut herring up and down the water column and is most often employed when targeting kings. My best mooching trip was out of Sitka, Alaska, with Jon Dale. We ran an hour to a particular island that held kings during the incoming tide. Lowering down our herring, we both took multiple big kings from this area which was no bigger than a basketball court. When you think the fish are in a certain area, it a fantastic method. The first and arguably most important step is to prepare the bait. Sometimes they are acquired locally. They are often purchased in neat trays that always seem to cost more than you think. I like to slowly defrost the baits and coat them lightly with salt to ensure they are firm and will not tear off the hook. Treat them carefully to not remove scales, which are key to catching the eye of a passing salmon. Once defrosted, they are plug-cut, which means cut at a forty-five-degree angle while holding the knife blade itself at a forty-five-degree angle. With a little practice it is easy and the angle will create the deadly slow spin. Before employing, remove the fish's entrails and also poke a tiny hole at the end of its abdominal cavity so water can escape.

The rig is simple: two octopus-style hooks on a three- to five-foot leader attached to a keel weight that can weigh anywhere from two to six ounces depending on the current. The bait is designed to spin, so ensure the leader has either a bead-chain swivel or a ball-bearing swivel. To hook the bait, the front hook is inserted up through the backbone, securing it in place. The rear hook is generally put once through the base of the tail and left to dangle.

To fish, the rig is slowly lowered to the bottom and, likewise, slowly retrieved up to the bottom third of the water column. Strikes are not violent, in fact usually quite the opposite. The line just gets heavy. The key is to resist the temptation to set the hook. Instead, keep reeling until it is obvious you have a fish on, then set the hook. Trolling and mooching are fun, but I really get excited when the salmon finally exit the ocean and start running up the rivers.

River Fishing for Silver Salmon

When I first moved to Kodiak, it was at the last breath of the red run, but just at the kickoff of the silver salmon run. Each trip I had to decide if I wanted to use my fly rod or spinning rod. I consider both my spinning gear and fly rod as tools; I love fly-fishing but not to the point that I will sacrifice catching fish to be a purist. There are times when it just cannot compete with eggs or lures, and I knew I brought the wrong tool to the river. Likewise, on low water days in August, conditions were not conducive to casting a big, flashy spinner, which seemed to scare away more fish then attract them, and the stealth approach of fly-fishing was ideal. A typical silver season will cover a large variety of river conditions, from near drought in the late summer to high water blow-outs following the first big storm of the fall. Each different river condition calls for a change in approach.

Low and Slow River Conditions

A few Augusts ago was marked by unusually low water conditions, combined with a massive number of pink salmon in the river systems. This warm, low oxygen combination made the fish congregate exclusively in the deepest holes of the river, discouraging the main body of the silver run from pushing up the river. It seemed like the ratio was 300:1 of pinks to silvers. There were silvers to be caught, but you had to fight through the pinks. I know this sounds like an exclusively Alaskan problem, having too many fish available. However, by this point the pink salmon have turned from their bright silver edible colors to various brown, gray, and olive hues. Unless you are very hungry, I wouldn't encourage their consumption. Conversely, the early silvers stand out in the river like giant chrome submarines. They will bite, but the key is to not let any pinks take the hook to avoid getting frustrated and likely breaking a rod.

My weapon of choice for low water is the fly rod. Except at dawn, this fishery involves a lot of sight casting, since I could watch the salmon follow and strike my fly. If it was a pink, I just let the fish bite, and then spit out the fly. If it was a silver, it got a solid hook set. In low water, the big flashy lures and flies are often too much for the warier salmon. A scaled-back fly in subtle colors that I can work through the deep holes, particularly on the incoming tides, is my best option for success. I really like baitfish patterns in this case, mimicking the candlefish found in the ocean. A fresh silver will still have a memory of these baits and seems to respond well to narrow, thin patterns.

Most classic salmon fly patterns involve big flies with bright colors. Because the fish are often not interested in feeding once away from the saltwater, these gaudy flies seem to elicit a strike out of either a territorial response or because they are just plain offensive. Using hot pink or purple rabbit fur or marabou creates a pulsing fly, similar to the movement of an octopus that they find appealing. Many of my best hand-tied flies were not based on a specific pattern, but a product of being creative with my materials. I was particularly fond of chartreuse marabou and would incorporate it into many of my patterns. These bright, brash flies even worked in the low water periods. To be successful, I would be down at the river before dawn, casting in the dark. With just a touch of light, the silvers, after relaxing all night, would freely strike these patterns. By the time the sun came up, however, the jig was up, and the bright colors were just too much to handle. It wasn't until the sun got low again or fresh rains came that the fish's attitude changed.

There are few other people besides the weather forecasters that pay so much attention to rainfall amounts as do river fishermen. Following a period of low water, having a big storm come through is great news. Not only will it clean out the rotting pink salmon soup that has been stinking up the rivers, but it draws in a big slug of silvers. The river will rise and perhaps be unfishable for a short period, but as it begins to show the first signs of dropping, that's the time that I stow the fly rod and break out the spinning rods.

To be fair, I have had some great success with high water fly-fishing. The technique known as "chuck and duck" involves weighted flies and sore shoulders, as brightly colored flies are sent out in the river to sink fast to meet the salmon hugging the bottom. This is when the hot pink and chartreuse flies really shine. Using a heavily weighted fly and working the current breaks and back eddies of the rivers is a good way to find fish. It is fun but something I wouldn't do if I wanted to fill a limit quickly. Additionally, if the fish got into the fast main current and headed downstream, it was usually a chore to muscle it back up river without breaking the line or pulling the hook out. Often, a more effective technique is to switch to salmon eggs or lures, as the scent or vibration gives the salmon a better chance to home in on your hook.

Eggs from any salmon species can be used to catch other salmon, but kings and silvers seem particularly interested in eating eggs. I prefer eggs saved from red salmon, since they are a smaller egg and seem to remain on the hook a little longer as a result. It's seems crazy when you think about it, but the hypothesis is that it reduces competition.

To fish using eggs, anglers will generally "cure" them, which entails quasi-preserving the eggs with a commercially made powder or borax, often with a powered dye included as well. I tried it but didn't love the side effects, including dying my cuticles florescent pink. In fact, I distinctly recall my boss flying up from the lower forty-eight to first meet me and I had to explain why the cuticles of my fingernails were hot pink. Non-fishermen just don't understand.

Silvers can seek out eggs in even the murkiest waters. I usually fish uncured eggs, mostly because of the aforementioned side effects, but also because fresh eggs work really well and require no work outside of drying them with a paper towel. They will last for about a week in the fridge, although if fishing is good, they shouldn't be in there too long. Add just enough weight to tick the bottom and gingerly lob out a quarter-size chunk into known holes. Regardless of the water clarity, eggs will draw any hungry fish in. Once a silver picks it up, don't be in a rush to set the hook; like mooching, let it come tight and set the hook once you feel the weight of the fish.

The downside of eggs is that you can't do too much exploratory fishing with them. If you are working an unknown stretch of river, it is time to tie on a spinner, spoon, or flatfish. The vibration, flash, and color in high water conditions are exactly what silvers are looking for. I had some great success with each of these lures. In all cases, I didn't have to do much more than keep the line tight and swing it downstream, allowing the current to impart the action as I maintained enough tension to keep it above the bottom. It is an effective way to cover water and get a feel for which eddies or sloughs are holding fish. Additionally, the strikes on lures are often explosive, as these fish take it as a personal insult that your lure swung past their face. Once I locate fish, it is often effective to switch back to eggs, as even the most patient silver cannot resist fresh eggs drifting by.

Silver season is a magical time. Each one is a little different, and to be successful, you must adapt to the prevailing conditions. If you exclusively throw spinners, eggs, or flies, there will be days that you just can't connect, and you will go home with as many fish as you started with. Stay flexible, read the river conditions, and if what you are casting is not working, try something new.

Fishing for Reds

Unlike the other four Pacific species, reds have unique needs that set them apart. Specifically, they generally need to spawn in a lake and spend their first years in that lake before heading out to sea. Although tending to be smaller than all but pink salmon, with the biggest one I have caught probably being nine pounds, they make up for it with incredible speed, huge jumps, and most importantly delicious flavor. I love standing still in a river and waiting for a formation of reds pushing up in shallow water; they are probably my favorite salmon to pursue. The gear is simple and the rewards are high if you have the patience. Getting them hooked can be the tricky part.

Where to Find Them

Reds are found throughout the state, from small Southeast streams, which may support a few thousand total fish, to the mighty Bristol Bay fisheries, which supports runs measured in the millions and supplies the world with canned salmon. This area is the backbone of commercial salmon fisheries for Alaska. It also supports a number of lodges that provide anglers an opportunity to fish these rivers as well and get in on the staggering amount of fish. Moving to the southcentral part of the state, the Kenai and Russian Rivers are the primary powerhouse systems for much of Alaska's residents and visitors. These rivers are easily accessible for the traveling angler by car, and although they can be crowded in the more popular spots, they can boast a very large and consistent run of fish. Further south, Kodiak supports a comparatively smaller run of reds for sport fishermen, as does much of Southeast Alaska. Again, the key to finding a good red salmon river is identifying a lake at its headwaters: the bigger the lake, often the bigger the run.

If you poll Alaskan salmon fishermen, the consensus is that reds don't bite. The ones that are hooked are "flossed," which means the leader is drifted through the fish's mouth and it is simply force fed. A fish hooked anywhere but exactly in the mouth is considered to be snagged and must be released according to regulations. I have gotten into boisterous arguments with friends on the topic of, "Do reds actually bite?" It best occurs over multiple drinks and with excessive hand gesturing. On days like the Fourth of July when a prodigious number of anglers stand shoulder to shoulder along popular rivers, I can't disagree that those fish, which are running a gauntlet of lead and steel, are probably not in the mood to strike a fly.

On the contrary, I have absolutely had reds take flies in the right conditions. For me, the right conditions are first thing in the morning, with no pressure on the river, and fish holding or swimming calmly. A cleanly swung fly past the fish has resulted in a clean hook up that could not have occurred by simply snagging them in the mouth. This is part of the reason why I like to be first on the river, to be able to cast to calm fish who are in the mood to bite. Brooks has even caught them trolling a bare red hook in the lake in which they are spawning. While I held subsistence salmon licenses, I never had a need to set a gill net or dip net for reds; I always caught enough for the family on my fly rod. Subsistence fly-fishing was my way of filling the freezer, and it felt good once in a while when I caught more than those using a gill net.

Rigging Up

Keeping it simple, I use ten-pound test Maxima line as my leader, which I make the length of the rod. Borrowing a tip from a friend, I position the split shots by placing the fly at the top of the cork handle and putting my weights at the second guide up. I am a big fan of non-lead spit shots and I use several size five weights to get it down to the proper depth—just ticking off the bottom. My fly choice is also simple, either an egg pattern or a small flashabou streamer tied onto a size two or four hook. I like using egg patterns because I can also pick up rainbow trout and dolly varden as well. But there have been times where I missed a red because a less desirable trout came charging in and hit the fly before it reached the salmon. A real Alaskan problem—wild rainbow trout taking a fly meant for a salmon!

Maybe I like red fishing because it has a component of hunting. Just like with silvers, I watch the river levels. I wait until it rains and the water begins to rise. Then when the level starts to fall, I head out, trying to pick spots to fish where I anticipate the fish will transit up, like a bow hunter setting up on a game trail. If the weather is "too nice," and not enough rain falls, I use the flood tides as a good indicator of when to hit the river, as the incoming tide will ferry in the fish.

Rather than beat the water for hours blind casting, I will stand and wait where I know fish will eventually pass through. The advantage you have over the fish is that it's their first and only time in the river and they tend to follow historical paths dictated by currents and, more importantly, water depth. If I think fish are pushing up the river system, I will stand in the same spot for hours, just waiting for the fish. It sounds painful and cold, but patience is the key, and standing knee-deep in a river is about the most relaxing place imaginable. I have had river otters swim past me, foxes come check me out, and have listened to eagles circling overhead.

It never gets old, but it will eventually get cold. Staring at the water, I tend to zone out and as my eyes become accustomed to objects moving downstream; but a school of fish moving upstream will catch my eye. Then I can transition to making a good cast without spooking the fish. I place the fly well above the fish. The key is to drift the fly motionless through the fish, following your fly with your rod tip and waiting until it comes tight. There is no better feeling than having your fly stop and then seeing a big red shake its mouth, indicating that it has taken a fly and is trying to expel it, before coming out of the water trying to shake the hook from its jaw.

Many rivers, especially those that support big runs of red salmon like the Russian and Kenai, are deep, fast, and glacial-fed. In these rivers, it is nearly impossible to see the fish. Additionally, you may find yourself with a few (hundred) fellow fishermen joining you as well. So fly-fishing with a few small split shots will not do the trick. This is the time when I like to leave the fly rod behind and bring out a spinning or bait casting rod and reel combination.

I have had great days on the Russian River with my dad and brothers, catching our limits simply by modifying our technique. We went with eight-foot medium action rods with bait-casting reels. Instead of a few small spit shots, a small egg sinker weighing a quarter to a half an ounce was required to maintain contact with the bottom. The heavier tackle also helped control the fish before it ran down through a lot of other lines. Many areas like the Russian have specific hook requirements, so check the regulations before you go. The concept is the same though—you just do it without seeing the fish. Work on swinging your fly through the river, keeping it just above the bottom. It helps to visualize your weight and fly to keep the weight brushing just above the bottom. When you come tight on a fish, there is no nibble, just a big strike as that fish takes off.

Targeting reds can take some practice, but the rewards are worth it. Unlike other salmon species, they don't hang out too long in one spot, but they do have a patterned way of swimming and resting as they transit up the river. I once had a very large school come by me. I was fortunate to hook a fish, but the remaining ones kept pushing upriver as my fish took me downriver. After landing it, I got into my car and drove a mile up the river. Sure enough, I had the school come by me again as I took my second fish to complete my daily limit. Take some time to study the river and select a choice spot. After a long winter, the first sign of summer for me is the arrival of the reds. Their bright, neon-red flesh is as satisfying to the eyes as well as to the palate. Enjoy these fish, but treat them with a high level of reverence—they had a long and complex journey to make it back to the river.

Halibut

My halibut gear is the same as my New England cod fishing gear. In all my days of halibut fishing, including hooking some sea monsters of this species, I have never had a fish tangle me in the bottom, cut me off, or spool me, so I have continued to downsize the tackle I use. Common halibut outfits are more suited for tuna, with Penn Senator 4/0 reels and stout rods as the norm. This level of big game tackle is not needed. As for my rod and reel combo, I really enjoy using an outfit that is light enough to hold in one hand all day. My trusty and go-to lightweight yet tough combo is a five-foot, eight-inch Penn Torque jigging, teamed with an Avet LX reel and sixty-five-pound braid. Regardless of your rod and reel choice, the key is to use braided line. With near zero stretch and very thin diameter, braided lines allow you to fish lighter sinkers and also feel each and every tap of potential bites.

Like the rod and reel choices, most commercially available terminal tackle for Halibut are tied on two- to three-hundred-pound test leaders with two monster circle hooks, to complement the oversize rod and reel combo that looks like it belongs on the back of a tow truck. It is a lot of firepower, and this is coming from a marlin fisherman. Fishing two hooks often leads to more tangles and excessive use of bait, but rarely more fish. My preferred halibut rig is a simple, single-hook dropper rig. These homemade rigs tied on comparatively light 80- to 150-pound test line positions the hook approximately eighteen inches off the bottom and rarely tangles. To sweeten the deal, I like to add a small glow-in-the-dark squid skirt above a medium-sized circle hook as a teaser. It adds a flash and color and seems to increase bites. The circle hook does not have to be huge, usually a hook in the 12/0 to 16/0 range is plenty, just ensure that it is razor sharp. Remember not to set the hook when using circle hooks either, something I forget to do once in a while. A circle hook is a self-setting one and will nearly always find its way to the corner of a fish's mouth as long as the angler slowly reels and does not pull the hook back. To control myself, I will often keep the rod in the holder during the bite so I don't mistakenly rip the hook away from the fish. I finish off the rig with the lightest sinker I can get away with, usually in the eight- to twelve-ounce range.

When choosing bait for halibut, freshness is more important than type for me. Fresh bait will stay on the hook longer and provide more scent, regardless of what it is. In depths well over two hundred feet, reeling up the weight to check to see if the bait is still there can get old fast. The best bait is one that stays on forever, and therefore my all-time favorite bait is octopus. I remember the day when Josh and I caught a giant Pacific octopus while halibut fishing. We used it for bait that day, as well as many trips after, and we put some serious fish in the cooler that season as a result. Unlike using chunks of herring, there is no way that a fish can pick a piece of octopus off the hook; it is hard to even wrestle it off the hook at the end of the day.

But if all you have available is frozen herring, that is perfectly fine, too, just be aware that it is easier for halibut or other fish to strip it off, so check your bait after each hit and gently lower it down as well. One tip that might help is to salt the herring before you use it. The salt will toughen up the often-mushy fish by pulling out moisture, and will therefore keep it on the hook longer. In many places, herring can be jigged up in harbors. Also, assorted bottom species like sculpins or greenlings can be caught while out on the halibut grounds. It is hard to beat the real deal—gently hooked in the back and lowered down—but be sure to verify in the Alaska fishing regulations what species can and cannot be used as bait.

What makes certain fishermen seem to have all the luck when it comes to a fishery that at first glance does not seem to have many tricks up its sleeve? It is not bait type or using special glow-in-the-dark jigs. Rather, it is the only thing that fishermen and realtors have in common.

Location, location, location! To me, it is the single most important aspect of chasing halibut, or really any bottom fish. Even with the best bait, you cannot catch fish that are not there. Halibut are ambush predators and will position themselves in an area that they know will have a food source nearby. More important than depth, tidal stage, or distance offshore, a contoured gravel bottom is what I key in on. Providing a smooth and clean surface to lie on, gravel bottoms support a productive array of feed, and the contours allow for perfect ambush sites for a halibut to lie and wait. Depth sounders and even charts don't always provide the clues needed to identify this bottom type, but one trick I use is to take note of what else is biting. If I am getting lingcod or rockfish, I know it is a craggy, rocky bottom and I will shift away until I stop catching those species. Likewise, if your bait comes up looking dirty, the bottom is often mud, which I have not had much luck with when pursuing halibut. My go-to spots are gravel areas, which fluctuate in depth by twenty to forty feet and are adjacent to rocky areas. The nearby rocks will support an array of habitat for bait to find safety in and the halibut will often lie down-current of these areas on the gravel waiting for feed to either swim to or depart from the rocks. These spots will be more productive during certain tides, so when trying a new spot, try it on a few different tidal directions until you know what is the most productive.

Once I have a spot under the boat, my next decision is whether I want to drop the anchor or drift fish. It is the same conundrum I face when targeting groundfish in New England, but the answer is similar for both, as they each have their time and place. If the current is moving, I prefer to anchor. Positioning myself up-current of my intended gravel hump, I want the boat to settle just forward of the peak. This allows me to lower my rig down so that my bait is in the halibut's ambush zone. Precision anchoring is often a challenge in deeper water, but err on the side of being farther up-current than down; the scent of the bait will pique their interest and you can always veer out more anchor line to adjust the boat's location farther back.

Another good trick is to vary the weight of the sinker on each angler's line. By staggering the lines, you will reduce tangles and also provide input as to whether the fish seem to be under the boat or farther back. The same can be accomplished by fishing different sized baits. One safety note to keep in mind when anchoring—remember, you still have to get it unstuck. Anchoring in rocky areas without a plan can make retrieving an anchor nearly impossible. I will often attach my anchor line to the crown (the bottom where the flukes come together) of the anchor and then use a zip tie to attach the anchor line to the ring on the top of the shank. When I am ready to weigh anchor, I just need to pop the zip tie off with a hard tug and the anchor is retrieved backward, freeing itself in the process. Likewise, on rough days, be careful of attaching the boat to the bottom as it can be a recipe for a really bad experience.

Drift fishing is my go-to technique on tide changes. I have found myself, on occasion, fishing on completely calm days, with no wind and in light currents. With no current to distribute the scent of my bait, slack tide is a great time to drift with what little wind or current exists to actively find fish. I have even bumped the engine in and out of gear to cover a bit more ground on those longer slack tides. This prospecting also helps me find new spots, as I may inevitably drift over the new honey holes and can mark them on the GPS for future trips. Drift fishing is also when I like to swap out bait rigs for jigs. Dragging heavy sinkers across the bottom usually doesn't end well and I never felt the bait looked natural either. A hopping twister tail jig enhanced with a strip of bait looks far more natural and has resulted in some good days for me.

How to Ship Fish Home from Alaska, Hawaii, or Anywhere Else

The downside of the fishing the wild waters is that they are often not close to home. After your catch has been properly processed and vacuum sealed, the journey isn't over until it is back home in your freezer. Here is how to do it right so those delicious memories last for a while in the freezer.

The first decision is to determine what type of container you are going to transport your fish in. The two main options are a fish box or a cooler. There are pros and cons to both.

Fish Boxes: Available throughout Alaska, a fish box is a strong, often waxed cardboard box that is used to ship perishable items. Usually rectangular, they are measured in the amount of product they can fit, with twenty-five-pound and fifty-pound boxes being the most popular. Relatively inexpensive, they are a quick and easy way of packing up the protein for the trip home. When using a fish box, ensure that it comes with a liner. A liner is generally an insulated bag that prevents outside air from coming in contact with the fish and will extend the time the fish can remain in transit.

Coolers: These are my preferred container for frozen fish, mainly because they are more insulated, rugged, and reusable. They are also a little less conspicuous and don't advertise the contents as much as a fish box does. A standard cooler will also fit about fifty pounds of product as well. This is an important number because many airlines will consider anything over fifty pounds as an oversize item and will at least charge you more, if not make you remove weight. What I like about coolers is that there is thick insulation within the walls that will keep the fish colder longer. To prolong the cold, I like to place the entire cooler into a walk-in freezer, if available, before I pack it full of fish. This draws the room temperature air out of the insulation before the fish goes in. If a big freezer is not available, I will at least place frozen water bottles inside the cooler ahead of time, again to cool it off before the fish is packed.

Regardless of using a fish box or cooler, the key is to pack it as tight as possible with fish. This means positioning each piece so that minimal air exists between the bags. The dead air space is what will begin to defrost the fish. After the fish have been loaded into the box or cooler, be aware of what is on the top, as it is most likely to be the pieces to defrost first. I will often use frozen gel-packs or something similar to be the sacrificial top piece to protect the fish underneath. Otherwise, plan on eating the top fish first.

Once tightly layered with frozen fish, it is time to wrap the cooler or box tightly with heavy duty tape, a task best done by two people. If the cooler was in the freezer, it will have condensation on it, so give it a moment and wipe it dry so that the tape sticks. Ensure the wraps are laid flat and be sure your name is visible on the box or cooler.

You can either ship the fish home by paying for a commercial carrier like FedEx, or bring it on the airline as checked baggage. If I am traveling home, I will usually check it as luggage. This way, both the fish and I arrive home at the same time and I can safely pack it away in the freezer with a deep sigh of relief. It is a relatively hassle-free way of bringing the fish home.

I like to use a commercial carrier when I need the fish to arrive before or after me. An example might be that I have multiple boxes and I want to get one out ahead of myself early. Having done this in both Hawaii and Alaska by using the fastest possible option, the fish arrived still frozen on the east coast of the United States. It will cost more, but with tracking, it is a safe bet. Just be sure someone is waiting on the other side to receive and pack the fish away for you.

Airports in Alaska are used to shipping frozen fish and many actually have cold storage spaces to keep the fish boxes and coolers in as well. Roughly speaking, the fish, if properly packed, will stay frozen for twenty-four hours. This is more than enough time to get it to most places around the globe; modern logistics are an amazing thing. Only once have I had my fish lost. It arrived a day later and it was defrosted, but thankfully, still cold. I ended up eating a lot of king salmon that week as re-freezing previously defrosted fish doesn't result in a great product. It is doable, but not ideal.

An obvious step, but one that is sometimes overlooked, is to ensure that you have sufficient freezer space to accept fifty or one hundred pounds of fish. Most of our kitchen freezers do not have an extra fifty pounds of space available unless some forethought has gone into it. In my basement I have two chest freezers. They are not always plugged in, but they allow me to pack away hundreds of pounds of fish should I need to. In the weeks leading up to a big trip, I will turn them on and ensure they reach the correct temperatures. I did this check once and determined that one had broken since the last time I had used it. Luckily, I was able to get a replacement before I left. It is important to have them running when you get home, ready to keep those fish bags cold as they come out of the cooler. I like to use reusable shopping bags to organize my fish species. This way I can sort out how much I have, and how much I am using. Dumping it all into a large chest freezer makes it hard to see what is really in there, and how much you have left. The shopping bag technique also prevents fish bags from getting lost in the bottom of the pile and never used. I don't like to keep fish for more than six months. Most of our nonindustrial freezers cannot achieve temperatures to freeze the lipids (fats) present in fish like salmon and tuna. As time passes, those lipids begin to break down and will cause off tastes. Fish is not a fine wine and it is best to not defer the happiness of eating it.

There is a deep satisfaction that comes with eating wild protein from wild waters, harvested by your own hands. With a little bit of pre-planning, the logistics of getting the fish home is straightforward. Pack the fish tight, no air pockets, and fill in any gaps with frozen gel packs. Duct tape the box tight and get to the airport early to ensure it makes the flight with you. Opening a cooler of hard frozen tuna, salmon, or halibut back home is a feeling of personal pride, as are the many meals that follow it. Enjoy.

Appendix Five

Hawaii

Trolling Island Style

U nlike nearly anywhere else I have fished, when trolling Hawaii, the next bite could be a thousand-pound fish. Heavy gear is not always needed but, eventually, a fish of a lifetime will enter your spread and you must be ready for it. It doesn't matter if your lures are small, or you aren't targeting big fish. They will find you, and it is a real heartbreaker if you are not ready. There are monsters out there.

For trolling outfits, reels and their corresponding rods are graded out by the original size of monofilament they were designed for. An example is a 130-class reel, which was designed to be spooled with 130-pound test line. As far as the reel sizes, like rifle calibers, they are on a spectrum. On the far-right end of the spectrum is the 130s, the elephant gun. These are the biggest reels created and represent your best shot of landing a fish of consequence, whether it be a thousand-pound marlin in Hawaii or the same size tuna off of Massachusetts. The reel classes drop down from there with 80s, 50s, and 30s being the popular sizes. A larger reel affords two things: more line capacity and higher drag ratings. Line capacity in a sense represents time. If a fish is making a long run, you only have so much time to either slow the fish or turn the boat around. Even on my highly maneuverable boat, I had hundreds of yards of line out before I could turn on my big marlin; 130s are overkill until the moment you hook "the one."

With the creation of braided line, a lot of these reel classes are now spooled with braided line backing and then a "top shot" of monofilament. When trolling in Hawaii on my boat, I typically run two 130s and two 50s. The 130s had 200-pound test spectra backing and 150-pound test monofilament top shots. The 50s had 150-pound test spectra backing and 100-pound test monofilament top shots. Even with the slightly smaller 50s, I never took the rods out of the holder when fighting a fish unless I had to shift rod holders. It was a safety issue, as a small, rocky boat is a hard platform to put a fighting harness on to stand up to fight a fish. Also, I wanted the fish to fight the full weight of the boat. I preserved my strength as the fish pulled several tons of fiberglass around. For me, this was not sport or a game. I learned enough lessons the hard way to know not to be foolish.

Most all boats come with rod holders but none are reinforced. Trying to battle a large fish from one with high drag settings will result in the fiberglass surrounding the rod holder to cave in. To mitigate this, you can buy metal backing plates, but correcting this is an easy DIY project for anglers. From Jim Rizzuto's famous book *Fishing Hawaiian Style*, I got the idea of homemade backing plates. I bought a board of one-by-ten mahogany to act as a backing plate, which fit perfectly under the gunwale.

Each rod holder got a one-foot section, cut to the individual rod holder angle. If I was to do it again, I would try to keep the board whole, so that it would provide even more of a strong back. I also replaced the factory wood screws with stainless steel bolts, washers, and anti-backing nuts so the mahogany was tight against the fiberglass. I installed two ninety-degree swiveling rod holders as well, one on each side. This allowed my rods, which are all bend butts, to track the fish as it changed direction, an important feature when fish start running in multiple directions. Inside the fiberglass of the gunwale, I cored out the foam and replaced it with epoxy. This ensured the fiberglass was rigid and solid. With a bead of 5200 marine sealant, which is about the strongest adhesive known to man, the boat would rip in half before the rod holders gave out, which it nearly did once. If you do not have swivel rod holders but want a quick way of making them, drop a golf ball into a vertical rod holder. Your rod will be able to freely pivot on top of it.

Selecting Lures

Picking a few lures to run seems simple at first glance. Some have flat faces, some conical, but within the minutia of each lure's design lies its purpose. They are beautiful, elegant tools and a smart angler will take a moment to consider their choices before splashing one.

Based on the skirt size, there are three main lure sizes I use in Hawaii: nine-, seven-, and five-inch lures. The size is related to length of the skirt and not the overall size of the lure. There is little doubt that the colors we humans see are not exactly what fish see, as fish have a different number of rods and cones in their eyes than we do. However, decades of trolling experience have informed fishermen that the color choices do impact a fish's decision to strike a lure, and in Hawaii, skirt choices are a big deal. Moreover, certain species seem to show an affinity for certain colors. When employing rubber skirts, most lure heads carry at least two, and occasionally three, skirts. Selecting two skirts that complement each other and match the lure head is the art and fun of it all.

Skirting your own lure heads gives an angler the choice to either match a prey species with a natural pattern-type skirt or make a wild combination that looks like nothing found in the sea. I enjoy the challenge of staring at a wall of skirts and picking the two best options that complement a particular lure head. Creativity is often rewarded, but there are also tried-and-true skirt combinations that have stood the test of time and should be strongly considered. In Hawaii, lure skirting preferences differ from island to island, and even from leeward to windward on the same island. Blue over pink or blue over silver is a tried-and-true combination, and usually finds a home in many a spread. For mahi-mahi, I really like green over yellow and ono seems to have an affinity for black over pink.

Lure Shapes

Bullets

Bullets are about the most popular shape in trolling. It is simply a conical shape that tapers toward a point, mimicking the natural shape of most baitfish. Bullets are meant to be run subsurface, meaning that they do not normally ride on top of the water or splash much. Being shaped like an actual bullet, they are also hydrodynamic, which means they are stable and do not violently dance around either. These lures, which are not excitedly dancing around the wake, may sound boring and therefore unappealing but pelagic fish have a different point of view. Bullets are easily attacked; they don't get away. I have watched marlin come up and attack a marauding surface lure without success then turn and blow up a "boring" bullet. Likewise, if you are after ahi, a subsurface lure such as a bullet will be your ticket to success. I have one seven-inch bullet that has enticed marlin, mahi-mahi, ono, and tuna. If you were looking for a one-size-fits-all lure, bullets would be my choice.

Jets

If a lure is said to be "jetted" then it sports numerous holes running lengthwise through the lure. These pukas, (pipes or holes) allow water and air to be forced through them, causing bubbles, more action, and vibration. While any shape of lure can be jetted, it is often associated with bullets. Running jets gives a lure a bit more action than a standard bullet. I will troll jets in the same spots as I do bullets, but I particularly like them on the long corner position. The turbulence of the wake when combined with the shimmy of a jet looks really good; numerous fish agree with me, too.

Plungers

Plungers are the fun lures to run. They look exciting and their rhythmic action in the water is responsible for a lot of fish caught. With an angled or cut face, these lures are designed to attack the surface and then dive below, producing a beautiful bubble or smoke trail in the process as the air is pulled under. For a plunger to properly work, it must be positioned so that it can occasionally break the surface. This means that being used on the outriggers is my preferred location. Outriggers lift the line out of the water and create an angle so that the line does not touch the water until the leader.

Each time I set back a plunger I will get it roughly to where I want it and then make corrections so that at least once every ten seconds it breaks the surface. Using the Goldilocks theory, I don't want my plungers to spend too much time on the surface, potentially tangling, but a plunger that never comes up for air is not functioning as designed. One trick I employ off smaller boats is to use a small bird in front of the leader on plungers. A bird is a surface attracter, similar in concept to a flasher for trolling. With its "wings," it prattles atop the surface like a flying fish seeking flight. I attach them to the swivel of my main line, with the lure trailing about twenty feet behind it. The bird also helps keep the lure up near the surface so it runs properly. As the lure digs in, the bird will momentarily come out of the water and suspend in the air. It is a dead ringer for a fleeing flying fish, locally called a *malolo*. On a smaller boat like mine, a bird also ensures the plunger stays closer to the surface to occasionally grab a gulp of air. All species will hit plungers but they are my go-to for marlin and mahi-mahi. Both these species have a soft spot for splashing lures and heavy smoke trails.

The Spread

"The spread" is what is referred to as the entirety of lures you are trolling behind the boat. The lures, from the fish's view, represent a loose school of fleeing baits. To grasp this, pretend you are lying down on your back underwater and you watch your boat go overhead. First, most fish are not directly on the surface, they are at depth—could be five feet or, in the case of tuna, could be hundreds of feet. Remember, fish don't have eyelids and can't squint. So, if its high noon and bright, they will often go a little deeper than early in the morning. That's why cloudy days make great fishing days. But, back to our spread: Your boat goes overhead, note the churning prop wash. It mimics surface commotion like feeding fish. Then picture seeing a half dozen bubble trails in chase, and way back, a lone bubble trail. The first or closest lure to the boat is referred to as the "short corner," and it is often the lure that will get hit by the largest marlin, so plan accordingly. Large marlin are not intimidated by the boat and will come in to investigate the churning props and propeller wash. I, likewise, have had mahi-mahi and ono come right up to hit this position as well.

Next is the long corner, which will be from the opposite side of the boat and slightly aft of the first lure. I like putting seven- or nine-inch jet or bullet heads in this position. The perfect spot to position the lure is right where the white water from the wake ends. To keep the lure in the water with no chance of breaking the surface and getting lost in the wake, I will attach the line to a rubber band or release clip attached to a cleat. This location is out of the majority of the turbulent wake, but close enough to gain some action from the churning water and bubbles. A subsurface lure in this spot will stand out and catch the attention of any fish interested in the wake itself. This is the position that my 611-pound marlin was caught in.

Next to pass over you are the lures on the outriggers. There is the short rigger and the long rigger. Here I put my varsity lures, the ones that catch my eye the most. Keep in mind that to that marlin, at first glance, whether you go with a root beer skirt or blue ice with pink flakes, it looks about the same—a white bubble trail. It is not until the lure has the fish's attention and it gets a clean look at the bait that the colors seem to matter. On the short rigger I like to use a nine-inch plunger with a small bird in front. Plungers, by design of their cut face, will rise to the surface to momentarily splash before diving below again, leaving a trail of bubbles in the process. A plunger behind a bird looks a lot like a pair of flying fish that are trying to flee. On that spearfish I caught, the bird had scars from being "windshield wiped" by the fish's bill, before switching to the lure. This short corner position is where most of my marlin action occurs.

The long rigger is run farther aft of the short rigger and again is also a good spot for a plunger. Being more on its own out there, I like a very clean and frankly pretty lure that will pass inspection by a curious fish. Finally, behind it all and bringing up the rear is the shotgun. Long after the bubbles have dissipated, this lone lure passes by. If the fish are boat shy, this will be the lure to get the hit. I like to run a small bullet in this spot. Out on its own, a small bullet in the seven- or five-inch category is an easy target for any predator. This location is fun because the species are so unpredictable, the strike could be a marlin or a large needlefish, both of which I have caught there. It is also another spot that I like to run a bird from. Besides drawing attention to it, the surface action of the bird also helps me know where it is, which is useful when approaching a bird pile or floating log.

I always envisioned that a marlin just came up at full speed and blasted a lure. While this does happen, with the advent of underwater cameras, we now have a better view of how a fish responds to a lure. From what I have seen, a marlin will come up to a lure lit up, with equal parts suspicion and curiosity, and spend some time checking it out. It is almost like they know this isn't quite real, but they can't help themselves, like visiting Santa at the mall. This is where you want to have a good-looking, well-running lure and why I feel Hawaiian-created lures are so successful. These fish are getting a great view of this lure, and if it's not acting like its alive, the fish will pass.

Rigging Offshore Lures

Fish are won or lost in the garage. Long before a troller takes on hundreds of pounds of ice or sets out the five perfect lures into the spread, the preparation put into your tackle and leaders will often determine what the outcome of the strike and fight will be. Each lure, based on its size and action, should be rigged in a specific manner to ensure it fishes correctly. The choices you make between the swivel and the tip of the hook are where you want to spend some time to guarantee that it is correct and solid. When you inevitably hook into that monster marlin or triple-digit tuna, the confidence of a well-rigged lure is crucial when the fight turns from minutes to hours. For that reason, it is worth getting into some pretty detailed descriptions, right down to the gnat's ass, of how I rig lures. But with realistically limited opportunities to get a shot at something big offshore, it's worth having done your homework. If it goes wrong, take it from me that you will have plenty of time to dwell on it after the fact. But if you do all your preps, you may have a lot less of those remorseful reflections. Here is how I like to rig my offshore lures for success.

Leaders

Leaders are either designed to scale down the diameter of the main line, as in the case of fly-fishing, or increase the size of the line, in the case of offshore fishing. I tend to make the length of my leaders longer as the diameter gets bigger. For smaller lures like a five-inch, I usually rig on 150-pound test and below, and I keep the leader length around twelve feet. It gives me a healthy distance between my swivel and the lure, while allowing me to leader and gaff a smaller fish by myself. For my larger lures rigged on either 250- or 300-pound test, I go a minimum of two and a half arm lengths, or about eighteen feet. In anticipation of a large billfish or tuna, I want to ensure that the fish's tail will never touch the main line. It also allows me to trim a foot or two off the leader, should it get chafed by teeth or a marlin's bill, without throwing the whole leader out.

As for actual leader size, it should be scaled to the lure, but the Hawaiian fisherman in me also likes slightly heavier leaders because you never know what the next strike might hold. A quick sea story on leaders: A while ago, I was trolling a small feather jig on twenty-five-pound test, off of Ka'ena Point, trying to catch aku, which were schooling on the surface. The long rigger took a strike, which quickly came off, but I could see a shadow of a fish out there. I teased it in the shadow and sure enough, of all the options, it struck the small bait lure on twenty-five-pound test. Whatever it was, likely a large marlin,

I couldn't keep it on for long. If I had my usual 100-pound test aku lure out, I feel confident I would have had a decent shot at landing that fish. Which leads me to my point: unless the smaller fish are finicky, for a five-inch skirt targeting smaller tuna, 100- to 150-pound is great. As I move into the seven-inch lures, I go with 250-pound test, and finally for my big nine-inch lures or if I am live trolling a small tuna, I go with 300-pound test. My preferred leader type is Momoi X-Hard and I use Momoi's oval crimps to hold the leader together.

Hook selections and placement is the fun part of rigging offshore lures. Each lure I run has a deliberate hook choice and position based on the lure's size and targeted species.

Double Hooks

Doubles look like a two-fingered claw, and are my go-to choice when I am chasing tuna or ono, and when I am trolling subsurface lures, either bullets or jet heads. But, after a few positive experiences on Pat Murphy's boat using double hooks on plungers to land marlin, I am really sold on these hooks for nearly every lure. Once both hooks dig in, they rarely come out. Much like safety chains on your boat trailer, the stability and balance of two points of purchase ensures even, constant pressure as the fish turns and jumps. As for hook placement, both these species of fish seem to hit more forward on the bait, so I look to have the hooks sit about two-thirds down the bait, facing upward, so the hook will come into the fish's mouth. I haven't had any issues with the skirt tangling these hooks either. Small doubles are also my go-to on my smallest lures. Whether it be a small tuna or a mahi-mahi, these small hooks just don't let go. My biggest mahi-mahi to date, a fifty-pound bull, was on a small five-inch lure with a small double hook.

Tandem-rigged Single Hooks

This is the standard choice for most seven- and nine-inch surface and subsurface runners. I make the tandem rig by crimping a Mustad southern and tuna hook as close to the head of the lure as I can. I then use 300-pound test leader to go from the eye of the first hook down to the bottom of the skirt and set it, so that the trailer hook's bend is just beyond the skirt's tips. I make my trailer hook one size smaller than the front hook. If I have an 8/0 in front, I want a 7/0 or 6/0 in the back. Also, be sure to use chafing tube on that piece of mono to ensure it doesn't get worn through as can happen with salmon trolling. Rather than shrink-wrap it and risk the heat weakening the mono, I borrowed a trick from Pat Murphy and use a small zip tie to fasten the mono to the leading hook. I like to have my hooks either 180 or 90 degrees offset. This means that both hooks are not oriented exactly the same, so depending on the direction of the strike, the fish will find at least one hook point. I like to keep the rear hook loose so it can swing and "gaff" the fish if it initially gets pinned to the top hook. In fact, some guys call the rear hook the gaffer just for that reason. This is often how marlin will be hooked. They strike the lure's head with their bill and get caught by the rear hook in the process. The downside to the tandem hook rig is that it can be a nightmare if you swing a fish (mahi-mahi are the worst culprits) onboard and it goes crazy.

I have a friend who took the rear hook into his abdomen as he swung a mahi-mahi onboard, and the fish did a number on him.

Single Hooks

Single hooks are becoming more popular for rigging. For guys who exclusively target marlin, I often see just a single hook generously exposed out the bottom of the skirt. The reasoning is that a marlin is tough to hook on a good day and, going back to the gaffer hook concept, a hook hanging outside the skirt will often be in a position to grab the fish. Having lost more than my share of marlin on tandem rigs, I am beginning to make the switch myself for my larger lures.

I also like a straight single 8/0 hook on my seven-inch plungers, cut faces, or any lure that will break the surface. These lures are relatively small, and with the rigged hook toward the back so the legs of the skirt can't tangle the hook, it provides a good hook set and looks clean.

Positioning the Hook

I have tried a few different options for positioning a hook a certain distance from the head of the lure, from using beads, to crimps, to plastic tubing. I found that beads have a reaction with the skirt and turn sticky; crimps are ok, but I don't like adding any more pressure onto the leader than I have to. The winner for me is my old friend, stiff, clear chafing tubing. It protects the leader, doesn't react with any other plastics and won't fold over. To hold the hook in position I have played around with using a toothpick to pin the leader inside the lure head, but have since gotten away from it. The lures I run are homemade and ballasted so that they run upright. Before putting the bait into the spread, I position the hook how I want it and gently lower it into the water. The lure and hook usually sit perfectly. One note: be sure to use a piece of that same chafing tube through the head of the lure. I melt one side of the tube with a quick touch of a lighter so it mushrooms out and stays in place. The piece prevents the metal tubing within the lure head from scoring the line, which I have seen occur.

The Key to Success

Of all the nuances I've already mentioned, there is one that is even more important and that is the sharpness of the hook. I am obsessive about hook sharpness and a high-quality sharpening stone is an important investment. If you look closely at an offshore hook, there are five distinct edges to a hook. To sharpen them, place the sharpening file or stone on each flat face at a moderate angle and slide it toward the tip. Doing this for each side creates a symmetrical point. A sharp hook should feel sticky to the touch. Even if a fish didn't hit the lure, it is worth touching up a hook after each trip.

Lure rigging sometimes feels like taping the edges of a big wall before painting. It is not necessarily the fun part, but it is the key to success. Each load-bearing connection between the fish and the main line needs to be well thought out, strong, and checked often. Losing a big fish is always heartbreaking and although there are many reasons for that happening, a dull hook or chafed leader shouldn't be among them. Dedicating time in the off season to making each rig perfect will give you one less thing to worry about when that monster marlin crashes the spread.

Appendix Six

How to Care
for Your Catch

Once the decision to harvest a fish has been made, crucial steps need to be followed to ensure the fish is taken care of ethically and will be safe to eat from a food sanitation standpoint, as well as ensuring maximized taste potential. If you have ever described a particular cut of fish as tasting "fishy," you have likely had an experience with poorly handled fish. Quality tasting fish begins even before it is hooked.

A cooler and ice are a requirement for any fishing trip. Quickly cooling a fish down is important to mitigate bacteria growth and prolong quality. Even in a colder environment like

Alaska, it was imperative to ice down my catch and I went to great lengths to ensure I always had plenty of ice available before each trip. I might keep my salmon on a stringer in a cold river while I was afield, but back at the truck, I had a cooler of ice awaiting my arrival until I could fillet the fish. At a bare minimum, you need as much ice as needed to completely cover the fish. To maximize the impact of ice and prevent the need to carry unrealistic amounts, Hawaiian fisherman will mix salt water and ice until it is the consistency of a margarita. This icy saltwater brine will lower the temperature below freezing and rapidly cool even the biggest of fish. When fishing on my boat, I will often employ a fish bag. These insulated bags, which resemble a rectangular sleeping bag, come in various sizes and are very useful for storing larger fish. Best of all, they don't take up precious deck space like a large, rectangular cooler would because they can conform to less-used spots on a boat. I have a five-foot fish bag and keep it up on the bow where nothing linear can be stored. It is out of the way, and it is no problem at all if it gets wet. Best of all it can hold a lot of ice and fish.

While I cherish the epic battles and wild jumps of fighting a big fish, at the cellular level, the fish is expending all its energy stores and releasing every performance-enhancing hormone into its blood stream to free itself. As the muscles continue toward exhaustion, the cells shift from aerobic to anaerobic cellular respiration. The result of anaerobic energy production is blood lactate, known as lactic acid, and that acid does not taste good. The first and sometimes overlooked step to perfect tasting fish is to use tackle suitable to the species.

This is why running heavier tackle, whether it be large 130-class reels for tuna or a nine-weight rod for salmon is important. There is a subset culture within fishing simply termed "light tackle fishing," which is essentially the pursuit of fish using the lightest tackle possible. While it does display an angler's ability, it does not do the fish any favors, particularly if you intend to retain it. If you are looking for dinner, it might be best to leave the light gear at home.

Once a fish is landed, do all you can to prevent it from flopping on the ground or deck of a boat. This is easier said than done in the case of salmon or mahi-mahi, as they will go wild once they are out of the water, but look to control the fish as much as you can without hurting yourself. All that flopping around will bruise the meat. Being out of the water to a fish means being asphyxiated, as it cannot breathe and further increases its stress. To prevent the fish from feeling this stress and producing a chemical response to it, its brain needs to be turned off, either by being punctured or stunned. Both have the same effects; it renders the fish no longer conscious or brain dead. In this crucial moment, there is a small window when the fish stops struggling, but its heart is still beating. This is when it needs to be bled, what is referred to as "exsanguination." With a sharp knife and ideally a Kevlar glove on (remember the tuna incident), I cut the gills on both sides. With the fish's heart still pumping, it will push all that hormone-laced blood out of the meat before it has a chance to settle. To remove the blood is to remove a prime source of bacteria production since it spoils fast. In case of a species like tuna, the blood will actually feel warm due to the heat generated from the fight.

Once stunned and bled, the next step is to gut the fish. The abdominal cavity is also a large factory for bacteria production, as well as an area that will retain heat, both of which are the enemy of high-quality fillets. Once I know the fish is dead, I will run my knife down the abdominal cavity, careful not to puncture any organs. Removing all the guts and then the gills, I flush the cavity with water to ensure it is clean. Now it is time to ice the fish.

If possible, I strive to place the fish upright in the ice. This allows gravity to pull down any liquids and keeps the fish clean. I ensure ice is neatly packed into the body cavity and gill area to maximize cooling. At this point, I can take a breath—I have taken the proper steps to preserve the maximum potential of my catch.

I, like most fish consumers, used to assume that fresh fish was the best fish and believed that eating fish right out from the ocean was the highest quality. Except every time I did this, it wasn't the best tasting fish. Fresh fish that I put on the grill the same day I caught it curled up along the edges, was a little chewy, and did not taste as good as it should have. Conversely, there were many trips when I caught fish later in the day and rather then fillet them after dark, I left them in ice overnight. By allowing the fish to rest a day or two, the flavor became more pronounced and the texture was more buttery. These fillets were supple and tasted exceptionally good. It was not until I spoke with Andrew Tsui, a fellow fisherman and seafood quality advocate who founded the Ike Jime Federation, that I understood the reasoning why. It was because the fish has gone through autolysis. This is the natural enzymatic process that breaks down the muscles after rigor mortis sets in, and is also known as the "aging" process. While aging is normally associated with steak, it applies equally to other meats like fish. However, due to poor handling like not bleeding and gutting, we don't often get to reap the benefits of aging fish before it begins to go rancid. This is why it is key to complete the steps listed above. During the enzymatic process of autolysis, a by-product called glutamic acid is created, which provides a savory taste. Now, when able, I will let a fish rest overnight in ice before filleting, allowing rigor mortis to come and go. When the fish is again supple, like the moment you caught it, the time is right to fillet it.

Regardless of the size of the fish, most of my filleting is done with the same Dexter fillet knife. I keep it razor sharp and will sharpen it after each fish. With a sharp knife, all you have to do is let the knife follow the backbone and ribs, keeping it ever so slightly angled down. Using long strokes, the fillet will easily separate from the bones. One word of caution—try not to get freshwater on saltwater fish fillets. Due to the salt retention of fish, the application of freshwater will cause the meat to turn off-white and washed out; this is the flavor washing away. Try to just wipe away or spot clean any issues with a paper towel.

With the filleting completed, it's time to pack your fish. I feel comfortable leaving most fillets in the refrigerator for up to four days, while checking on it several times a day. During this time, I will use a paper towel to ensure no liquids are building up as this is how spoilage will occur. After this, and hopefully after enjoying multiple meals, it is time to freeze it. A quality piston-driven vacuum sealer is worth the investment. It took me a while to recoup the initial price, but the smaller sealers just were not doing the job. I tend to pack my vacuum bags in one-meal increments for the family and use fillets of equal size, so the cooking time will be consistent. Just be sure to pat dry the fillets with a paper towel before sealing to prevent any freezer burn. Vacuum sealing is straightforward and a good way to get kids involved in the process as well. Once sealed, it is time to pack them away.

I own two chest freezers. Both are not always on but it is good to have excess capacity should it be needed. When placing the bags into the freezer, space out the fillets to maximize air flow. Stacking all the fillets on each other with no air between will cause a long delay in actual freezing. Try to spread them around the freezer and then stack them once they are frozen hard. It is always a good practice to label each bag with the species and the date. It keeps you eating the first-in bags first. I use reusable cloth shopping bags to organize fish by species. This makes it easy to grab what you want and avoids bags getting lost in the abyss that is a chest freezer. I don't like keeping frozen fish for more than nine months, and ideally closer to three. It is a good excuse to get on the water often to keep a steady supply of fresh fish.

Being a successful fisherman extends beyond just the catch. If you choose to harvest a fish for the table, there is a responsibility that comes with it. You owe it to the fish to treat it with respect as you prepare it. Also, nobody cares more about your food sanitation than you. I really enjoy eating raw fish, so it is paramount to ensure all the proper handling steps are taken.

A line I like to use is that food ends in plastic wrap, it doesn't begin there. Closing that disconnect between a wild fish in the sea and the fillet on the table is something to strive for. Take the time to understand how to break down a fish and properly care for it. The key to unlocking the maximum quality of a fish resides with the angler. Enjoy.

Works Cited

Coleman, Tim. *Fishing Connecticut Waters: Reprints from the Fisherman.* Evansville, IN: MT Publications, 1988.

Davis, Tammy. "White King Salmon Greenbacks, Gustatory Preference and Genetics." *Alaska Fish & Wildlife News.* Alaska Department of Fish and Game website, October 2006. www.adfg.alaska.gov/index .cfm?adfg=wildlifenews.view_article&articles_id=244.

Geslani, Cheryl, and Kimberly Burnett. "Most of Hawaii's Commercial Seafood Is Imported, but Recreational Catch Tips the Scales Back." UHERO, June 20, 2013. uhero.hawaii.edu/most-of-hawaiis -commercial-seafood-is-imported-but-recreational-catch-tips-the -scales-back/.

Kurlansky, Mark. *Cod.* New York: Penguin Books, 1998.

National Oceanic and Atmospheric Administration (NOAA), Special Projects Office. "USEEZ: Boundaries of the Exclusive Economic Zones of the United States and Territories." *USGS Coastal and Marine Geology Program Internet Map Server,* U.S. Geological Survey. Accessed March 04, 2021. https://pubs.usgs.gov/ds/2006 /146/basemaps/useez/useezmeta.htm

"News Update: U.S. per Capita Seafood Consumption up in 2017 • Seafood Nutrition Partnership." Seafood Nutrition Partnership, December 13, 2018. www.seafoodnutrition.org/seafood-101

/news/news-update-u-s-per-capita-seafood-consumption-up-in-2017/#:~:text=The%20U.S.%20per%20capita%20consumption,a%20greater%20variety%20of%20seafood.

Rizzuto, Jim. *The Kona Fishing Chronicles: Lure-Making 101/102*. Self-published, 2010.

Rizzuto, Jim. *The Kona Fishing Chronicles: Lure-Making 201/202*. Self-published, 2015.

Shintani, Terry, and Claire Hughes, eds. *The Wai'anae Book of Hawaiian Health*. Wai'anae, Hawaii: Wai'anae coast comprehensive health center, 1991.